Taking the Time to Live

The Healing Voyage of Pato Feo

Ron Fugere

B&H Bennett &
Hastings Publishing

Bennett & Hastings titles may be ordered through booksellers or by contacting: sales@bennetthastings.com or writing to 2400 NW 80th Street #254, Seattle WA 98117

ISBN: 978-1-934733-72-1, paperback
This title is also available in e-book formats.

For Jason and Nicole

Ahoy cap'n Bill !

Taking the Time to Live

And so I breaks me anchor chain
Spent thirty years, tho' not in vain
Two hearts were one, but now undone
'twere mine to do, I would again

She asks if thar be someone else
I answers "aye, indeed, meself"
She asks me now to where I go
To her I say "where fair winds blow"

So many years we'd been adrift
We found no glue to seal the rift
Our blood's been let, our course be set
Methinks we'll heal, tho' hearts are rent

Me kids I tell to "plot your course"
"Seek to find not who you are"
"Choose instead who you would be"
"Wait not 'till days are few, like me"

And so I boards me humble ship
And set forth in search of bliss
Cast off the lines that hold the past
And trust I will not breathe me last

Hank on the jib, bend on the main
And set sail to ease the pain
First north and west, then south and east
Alone I go, alone I'll be

Me days be filled from dawn to dusk
Indulging in me wanderlust
Joy filled by nature's noble beasts
'Pon beauty my eyes do daily feast

Not knowing what the future holds
I'll stake a claim you may think bold
If on this trek from Earth I'm torn
Do not be sad, please do not mourn

Better life be joy filled tho' fleeting
Than trudge through life and call it living
Life has for us so much to give
Glad I am for taking the time to live

Part One

And so I breaks me anchor chain

Fifty laps of the sun, fifty earth years. It was a time to reflect on how I'd lived my life and how I'd live out my days. I was newly divorced, gainfully unemployed, and living on my boat. I know what you're thinking, sounds like a mid-life crisis, doesn't it?

For thirty years – all my adult life – I'd run with the herd, leading a very normal life. I'd had a comfortable home, an attractive wife and two wonderful kids, a couple of cars, a motorcycle, a boat, about a hundred channels on cable TV and beer or scotch to help me wind down at the end of another day spent at my latest miserable job and commuting in the stop-and-go traffic of "Pugetropolis." Sounds like the American Dream, doesn't it?

I had met Peewee, my wife, when I was twenty years old. She was my first love. We had lived together for a couple years and then tied the knot. I got married in an olive green polyester double-knit leisure suit! Hey, at least it wasn't powder blue. Fashion sucked in the seventies! In our early years together, we were pretty happy. We had the usual highs and lows you would expect of any marriage, but all-in-all I'd say we had more good days than bad. At least we were blessed with two wonderful, bright kids, Jason and Nicole.

Over the years, Peewee and I had gradually grown apart, losing sight of what few common interests and values we'd once shared. Despite our disagreements we managed to hold it together long enough to raise our children. (Nicole, our youngest, would graduate from high school that June). My life had become hollow and unrewarding. It's a common story.

Shortly after I met Peewee, I had taken a job just to pay the bills; it was just a job, not a career choice. But one job had led to another, usually for more money and responsibility. I was good at what I did and fairly well-respected. I'd often had good jobs; but about every three years I would find sufficient cause to hate my job and move on. (I have come to realize that I am a chronic malcontent. Give me the best job in the world and I can find everything wrong with it.)

I had put aside very little toward retirement and envisioned myself comfortably starving to death on Social Security. My best plan for retirement would be to die young. I had worked hard all my life but had only more of the same ahead of me; and after thirty years in the same line of work, I realized that I had never decided what I wanted to be when I grew up. I found I just couldn't do it anymore. Working for a "living" was killing me! I wanted to try something new, but I didn't know what.

In seeking a new direction, I quit drinking (!) and began volunteering with the Sailing Heritage Society, a non-profit organization which operates the schooner *Mallory Todd* conducting charity cruises to provide a respite for those who suffer from cancer or domestic violence.

My volunteer role was supposed to turn into a paying position, and my hope was that I could find a way to make a living doing what I loved most: sailing. "If you're doing something you love, you'll never work a day in your life." It was a bonus to feel I was doing something worthwhile.

It was then that life started to get interesting.

The strain of my ongoing unemployment added more tension to my marital situation. The specter of divorce reared its ugly head. When I raised the idea, Peewee cordially invited me to find another place to live. She didn't think I was serious about a divorce and was trying to call my bluff. I was not bluffing. George, the owner of the *Mallory Todd*, kindly offered to let me stay aboard until I could make other living arrangements.

It was time to take inventory. I had no job and no home, a car, an old Ducati motorcycle, my boat, and ten thousand dollars; the remainder of my savings after Peewee withdrew her half in a preemptive strike. In one of the bleakest moments of my life, I asked myself what had led me to abandon my familiar, comfortable life and quasi-career for an uncertain future, working for free and sleeping on someone else's boat?

Why a boat?

All my life I've been interested in boats and sailing. When I was a kid, I built model sailing ships from scratch. Growing up in the

Puget Sound region I was always exposed to the water, and whenever I saw a body of water I wanted to be on it.

My first sailing experience, when I was about nineteen, had been on a T-bird with my now-deceased friend "Hippie Doug." I loved it! The magic of a boat under sail gliding over water held me enthralled. Soon thereafter, I bought a sixteen foot American sloop. It showed me just how little I knew about sailing. After I sold that boat, my life had a long, dry spell without boats, but the longing never ceased; there were simply other priorities.

The years went by, and I was nearly forty when I eventually acquired a ten foot sprit-rigged dinghy to use at Herron Island, where Peewee and I had bought a cabin. I spent many days sailing around the island, often in conditions when a tiny, little boat like that should not have been out. I soon progressed to an eighteen foot Buccaneer sloop as my passion for sailing grew. I learned a great deal about the intricacies of sail trim while I honed my skills sailing Case Inlet.

My introduction to long-distance cruising had been on a twenty-seven foot Sun Yacht, the *Pamplonica*, which my best friend Daniel borrowed from his brother. We set out to spend three weeks sailing Puget Sound and the San Juan Islands on what we dubbed the "no booze cruise." Two hard-core drinkers on a boat for three weeks without beer (sailboat fuel)?! What were we thinking?! *Pamplonica* was as ill-prepared for cruising as was her crew. The starter on her auxiliary diesel engine worked sporadically, the compass was not mounted and most of its oil had leaked out, the depth sounder transponder was not fixed to the hull so we dangled it over the transom by its cable, and we had no proper charts, but we did have one of those cruising atlases; you know, the ones that state "This chart is not intended for navigation." We sailed from Port Orchard as far as Stuart Island in the San Juans, which is almost as far northwest as you can travel and remain in the waters of the contiguous United States. We then sailed south to Herron Island, where Peewee and I still had our cabin, which is almost as far inland as you can go and still be in salt water. Along the way we got lost in the fog, caught in a kelp bed, and ran into a rock. Our near total lack of experience and skill proved to be no obstacle to us having the time of our lives. That cruise planted the seed that would grow into a passion for cruising and ultimately lead me to a new way of life.

As the kids grew older, they lost interest in spending their weekends on the island. Peewee stayed home with them more often than not, and soon I was spending my weekends alone or with friends on the island, drinking myself stupid. I began to have a hard time justifying the cost of owning and maintaining a second home if it was only to be a "boys club". Reluctantly, I sold the cabin; my fortress of solitude.

To fill the void left by selling the cabin, I bought a Catalina 27 which I named *Laughing Wind*, for the flukey winds of the Puget sound which often seem to mock us. The summer after I bought *Laughing Wind* I took a month off work and set out on my first solo voyage. OK, the truth is that Daniel joined me on the outbound leg of my journey; he seemed to think I would need a babysitter. He was right. He had just returned from sailing to Alaska in his boat, *Vientos de Cambio*, and immediately set out with me. Together we set sail from Tacoma and cruised through the San Juans, the Gulf Islands, and Princess Louisa Inlet. Daniel jumped ship at Westview, British Columbia, and I continued solo to Desolation Sound. On that voyage I had discovered that cruising could be more than a mere vacation; it could be a way of life.

Daniel and I shared another adventure the following year. We had discovered that we had in our possession a chart for The Broken Group. It looked like an interesting group of islands, but we had no idea where it was. We checked the latitude and longitude and found that it was in Barkley Sound on the west coast of Vancouver Island. Since we had the chart, we had no choice but to go there. Need you have more justification?

This all brings me back to that dismal, hopeless moment when I found myself in front of a Shilshole Bay Marina bulletin board, posting a flyer to promote a *Mallory Todd* cruise to Alaska, a fundraising event I'd been helping organize. It was then I met a young man who probably saved my life.

Joe was posting a flyer to sell his boat. He expressed interest in our Society and our Alaska cruise. I asked about his boat. She was a Coronado 35 ketch, the *Alejandra*. I asked if he felt it would be adequate for a liveaboard. He assured me that it was indeed; he had lived aboard for about three years. I'd never sailed a ketch before, and asked if she could be sailed single-hand. He replied that he found her easy to handle alone. We made an appointment to go see his boat where she was moored on Lake Washington.

The next day Joe and I met at the marina and walked down the pier to *Alejandra*'s berth. As we approached her slip, my first impression was formed: she was a big, ugly boat. Those who are familiar with Coronados will agree that they are not the prettiest or sexiest boats ever built. This one had a center cockpit, very high topsides, and a big, ugly casting on the bow that reminded me of the nose of a boxer who had lost a few too many rounds. Additionally, *Alejandra* wore a poly tarp over her cockpit and a winter's growth of green slime on her deck and along her waterline; not the most appealing sight.

We ducked under the tarp and went below. She had a somewhat cramped but adequate saloon, a nice galley and head, a generous forward cabin, and a huge aft cabin. She had standing headroom throughout, lots of nicely oiled teak, and many brass lamps. I could see that she would meet my needs.

I braced myself and asked his price. He told me thirty thousand, about what one would expect to pay for an older, thirty foot plus sailboat at that time. I quickly did the math in my head. If I could sell my Catalina for, say, ten to twelve thousand dollars, together with what I had in the bank that would leave me eight to ten thousand short. With no job, I would have a hard time getting financing, let alone making payments. I explained my situation to Joe. He stood for a moment in quiet reflection, and then said he would take ten thousand dollars. My heart skipped a beat: there might be a way to make it work! Would he accept my Catalina and ten thousand? He said he was not interested in my Catalina and would accept ten thousand dollars. *A thirty thousand dollar boat for only ten thousand?* Suddenly, I became suspicious; was there something seriously wrong with her? I said I would have to have a sea trial and a survey, fully expecting him to say, "Ten thousand right now, take it or leave it."

Instead, he checked his calendar and we set a date for the sea trial. I would call around to arrange a survey. My hope growing, I asked to see the cabin again. The second time through, I could see the boat as my home.

A few days later we did the sea trial while making our way down to Lake Union, where she would be hauled out for the survey. We had little wind, but we were able to make sail just long enough for me to become familiar with the rig, and I was able see how she handled under power. We pulled into the boatyard owned and operated by the surveyor, and discovered that the forestay would have to be unrigged in order to fit her into their mobile lift. Then they managed to put the aft sling under the propeller shaft. Fourteen thousand pounds of boat resting on a one-inch stainless steel shaft! Great! Fortunately, it was not bent.

In between taking numerous cell phone calls, the surveyor was able to complete (?) his job. Note to self: Check references before choosing a surveyor. Fortunately, Daniel had joined the fun, and he and I were able to poke around and learn a lot about the boat while the surveyor did his thing. The boat was found to be in overall good condition, with no significant defects. The bottom was newly painted and there were no gel-coat blisters. The standing rigging was new, and she had a newer diesel engine with relatively low hours. A few simple things like servicing fire extinguishers, adding environmental placards, etc., would render her seaworthy. The survey placed her value at thirty-four thousand dollars.

With the survey complete, Joe, Daniel and I proceeded to the documentation office to consummate the deal. I gave Joe a check and we signed the papers. Joe had asked me to rename the boat, as he had named her *Alejandra* after his mother and might want to use that name in the future. Daniel and I had spent the previous evening discussing and rejecting various names. I decided to go with my first impression and christen her *Pato Feo*, the ugly duck. Like the children's story, she was destined to become a swan in my eyes. I now had a home and new hope for the future.

Chapter Two

It was a lovely spring afternoon when the newly-named *Pato Feo* and I set out on our maiden voyage from Lake Washington to Port Orchard, where I had secured liveaboard moorage at Sinclair Inlet Marina. My crew consisted of myself, Daniel and his then-girlfriend, Paula, the "flavor of the week."

Under power, we made our way along Lake Washington and into the Montlake Cut, heading west, toward Lake Union. We arrived at the Montlake Bridge as evening rush hour commuters passed overhead, forcing us to bide our time. The bridge tender eventually halted traffic and raised the spans so *Pato's* masts could pass beneath. It was twilight when we entered Lake Union. When we turned on the navigation lights, we discovered that the batteries were nearly dead. It seemed the alternator was not charging the batteries. We tied up at Morrison's fuel dock which was closed for the evening and pirated some electricity from their shore power so we could charge the batteries for a few hours.

With the batteries freshly charged, we continued on our way. As we approached the Fremont Bridge, we were scolded by the bridge tender for requesting a bridge opening on the VHF radio instead of sounding our whistle. As we approached the next bridge, the Ballard Bridge, we discovered that my "whistle," – the usual aerosol can of compressed air with a signal horn attached – was rather uncooperative. As the evening grew late we finally passed through Salmon Bay to the Hiram M. Chittenden (Ballard) locks, which would lower us to Puget Sound.

We pulled up to the small boat locks and waited ... and waited. Eventually we realized something was amiss and backtracked to the entrance, where we saw a sign stating that the small boat locks were closed for repair and directing all boats to the large boat locks. *Pato's* mooring lines were barely adequate for boat handling in the large locks, but we were allowed to proceed. As one of the lock tenders drained the lock to lower us, he shouted something about the railroad bridge. I had no idea what he was talking about, due to my less than perfect hearing. We were underway! As they opened the gates, we experienced a sensation not unlike being a turd flushed down the toilet. This pushed us rapidly toward the railroad drawbridge, which was lowered! It suddenly became clear what the lock tender had been shouting. Sailing vessels and low bridges are not a match made in heaven. The locks' powerful current was sweeping us downstream and it took nearly full throttle to spin the boat around and hover while the train passed, and then the bridge was raised. At last, we made our way out through Shilshole Bay and onto Puget Sound.

At first light the wind was blowing ten knots, a perfect breeze for a shakedown cruise, so we made sail. It was my first opportunity to see how *Pato* would perform under sail, and most of the day we simply practiced on various points of sail. We found the self-tending jib to be a joy for a crew that had been up all night. When going to weather, we found that by trimming or easing the mizzen we could balance the boat so she would sail herself.

While I sailed for a bit, Daniel and his "squeeze" went below for a "nap." In fact, they were busy breaking in MY bunk in the aft cabin! Shortly after they came back up on deck, grinning sheepishly, we heard a crash below. It seems that the mirror in the aft cabin, strategically placed to observe various cabin activities, had come loose and shattered all over the cabin sole. Daniel was able to verify the merits of its placement, and the mirror has since been replaced. I am pleased to say that he was right.

By the time we'd picked up the mirror shards, it was late afternoon, and we'd had enough fun for one day (some of us more than others). We proceeded into Port Madison, where we anchored for the night, had a bite of dinner, and turned in early.

Early the next morning we sailed down Agate Pass and into Port Orchard. We pulled *Pato* into her waiting slip and made her fast to the pier. *Pato* and I were home.

My slip was conveniently located in downtown Po-Dunk (Port Orchard). I was able to secure a storage unit right next door (some stuff you just can't part with). There was a post office, library and restaurants a short walk away. Within easy driving distance were many grocery stores, a hardware store, a couple of marine supply stores, and most conveniences I might need or desire. Visible from my slip was the clock tower at City Hall, which chimes every quarter hour. At 8:00 AM, noon, and 5:00 PM the bells play a variety of lovely tunes; a real treat. Port Orchard Marina is a beautiful nearby facility. Operated by the Port of Bremerton, it's sidewalk follows the shoreline and is lined with picturesque gardens, their plantings changed with each season. The *Carlyle II*, a 1917-vintage historic foot ferry and one of the few remaining vessels from Puget Sound's "mosquito fleet," provides passenger service to and from Bremerton across the inlet, and visible from my slip is the public boat launch ramp, which provides a constant source of entertainment. Come on, admit it, we've all laughed at some poor fool when he jack-knifed his trailer, backed off the ramp edge and got stuck, then yelled at his wife as if it was her fault. And anyone who has owned a boat has been that fool at least once. For other entertainment, there is also a community theater.

Although I'd never lived in Port Orchard, Daniel, Ed and Mary Jo, Jim and Charlotte, and many other friends and acquaintances lived in the area. Plus, I would soon discover that marinas foster a sense of community that is sadly absent in most of America. I'd had a taste of this on Herron Island and hadn't realized how much I missed it. I'd lived for nineteen years on a dead end street in Puyallup and couldn't name more than three neighbors. In Port Orchard I found the vestiges of a small-town atmosphere. Home sweet boat!

Chapter Three

It was 0400 hours (4:00 AM for you land lubbers) on the second morning I'd spent aboard and the muffled sound of a slowly running bilge pump crept into my consciousness. As it continued to run, I became alarmed; could one of my neighbor's boats be sinking? I swung down out of the bunk to check, and was shocked to find about a foot of water in the cabin! *My* boat was sinking!!! I could see my new home and life slowly going to the bottom.

The bilge pump had nearly drained the batteries, so I hastily retrieved the handle to the "Whale Gusher" manual pump and dashed topsides. It was not yet dawn and I was out on the poop deck, buck-ass-naked, frantically pumping. Wendy, another liveaboard, walked by on her way back from the shower and wondered at the apparition. What was that naked guy doing!? I can only imagine how it looked.

At first light I ducked below to slip on some clothes. The sight of water continuing to rise caused my heart to sink, in sympathy with my boat. I cannot even begin to describe the utter despair I felt at that moment. A short while later Mike, Wendy's husband, came by. "Are you sinking?" he enquired. "So it would seem!" I replied. "Should I get the gas pump?" he asked. "That would be good!" I exclaimed. A short time later – OK, it felt like a year – Mike returned with a Honda pump. We were soon pumping the water out.

The question arose as to where the water was coming *from*. I'd been so frantic to stem the flow that all I'd thought to do was close all of the seacocks. Mike asked whether it was salt or fresh water. The thought hadn't occurred to me. I reluctantly tasted the water. It was fresh! I then shut off the water supply at the dock, and we began to gain ground. A short while later we had pumped out all of the water, and Mike and I made our introductions. When I met Wendy later in the day, she had a rather strange look in her eyes. Can you blame her?

I spent a few days getting the last of the water out of all the nooks and crannies. The water had risen above the intake and flooded the engine, but since it was fresh water there was no serious damage. I discovered that all of the freshwater hoses were brittle and cracked after thirty years of service, and they had been poorly routed under the engine. Brilliant! Whenever a hose had sprung a leak, some previous owner had merely cut the offending hose, inserted a short pipe nipple (about an inch long), and secured it with a couple hose clamps. This, coupled with the high pressure from the marina's water supply had nearly put *Pato* on the bottom.

I began the laborious task of replumbing my boat. I rerouted all of the hoses properly and used the strongest hose I could find. I added a ball-valve below deck so I could shut off the water at night. One near sinking was enough, thank you! I also cleverly added another ball-valve which would allow me to backfill the thirty gallon water tank while hooked up to the dock's water supply. A few weeks later, the water from the tap started taking on an offending odor, not unlike that of rotten eggs. I had used the strongest hose I could find; the wrong kind of hose! I then had the joy and pleasure of re-replumbing the entire boat using food-grade marine hose.

Thus began my life as a liveaboard. I was to spend much of the next year repairing and upgrading many items that had gone undiscovered during the survey. I had to rewire much of the boat, a process that continues to date. I am forever trying to stem the flow of rainwater which seems to always find a path into the cabin. I replaced the weathered and crazed plexiglass of the port-lights with safety glass in the hope that I would never have to do it again. I added a second bank of house batteries, which more than doubled my storage capacity. As any boat owner knows, the list of things to repair is endless: for every item you cross off, you'll add two or three more.

As a documented vessel, it is a regulation that the vessel's name and hailing port be displayed. I had chosen a name and now had to choose a hailing port. Although I was living in Port Orchard, my ties there seemed insufficient. I'd been raised in Purdy, but had left there when I was about eighteen. I'd lived in Puyallup for nineteen years and raised my family there, but I'd left that life behind. Besides, there is no port at Puyallup. The only logical choice was Tacoma. I had been born in Tacoma's St. Joseph hospital, as were both of my kids. Tacoma it would be! With boat name and hailing port in hand, I went to the local sign maker and ordered vinyl letters. In a few days they were ready, and I carefully applied them to the transom.

I then arranged to have Jason and Nikki come out to "Po-Dunk" so we could officially christen *Pato*. I bought a cheap bottle of champagne which I put in an old sock to keep broken glass from flying everywhere. Nikki uttered the obligatory "I christen thee *Pato Feo*," and swung the bottle with all her might. There was only a loud thud and no sound of broken glass. She swung again … and again. Jason offered to do it. He swung as hard as he could at the bar joining the flukes of my thirty-five pound CQR anchor. This bar is about a half inch in diameter and made of steel. It bent! Still we had no broken glass. Now it was my turn to try. I brought to mind all the frustrations of the last few years, wound up and swung. That did the trick! She was officially *Pato Feo*.

As I was adjusting to living aboard I was also adjusting to living alone for the first time in my life. I was to find that I enjoyed my own company. I'd come to realize that one can live in a house full of people and still be alone; alone in a crowd.

I began to consider getting a pet. My dog, "Fred, the wonder dog" had died in the midst of my separation from Peewee. He had been a joy in our lives for about twelve years, and his passing had left a huge void. I've always considered myself a "dog person," but I didn't want a dog on *Pato*. I love going ashore nearly every day on my travels, but I didn't want to be forced to do so in order to find a place for my dog to do his business and fowl someone's beach or lawn. I considered getting a bird, like a parrot, but ruled it out. I'd never had a bird before and knew nothing of their care. Besides, it seems almost cliché having a parrot on a boat. What did I think I was: a pirate? What about a rodent like a hamster or gerbil? No, they have too short a lifespan and are easy to lose in a boat, with so many hiding places. How 'bout a reptile, like an iguana or a snake? They're not very cuddly. I even wondered about a tarantula or a praying mantis. Perhaps the obvious choice: a cat? They are cuddly, and they mew and purr. They are somewhat independent and low maintenance. Best of all they can use a litter box.

I knew that if I were to get a cat, it would need to be declawed. Picture a cat sharpening its claws on your mains'l! I decided that I would like a female because, well, I like girls; but it would have to be spayed so I wouldn't have to deal with her being in heat. I'd always thought that cats lacked personality and could be somewhat aloof, but it still seemed to be the best choice. I saw an ad in the *Little Nickel* classifieds for a cat, female, spayed and declawed, free to a good home. She met all my requirements. I made an appointment to go have a look. She was a three-year-old brown tabby, rather small and absolutely beautiful. I knew as soon as I saw her that I'd found my traveling companion. She was being given up by a kind young lady whose husband was overseas in the latest Gulf War and whose father-in-law, with whom she would be staying, was allergic to cats. With tears in her eyes she agreed to let me have her cat, "Stoner Kitty."

I decided the name would have to go. As a former cat hater, I'd always thought that the best and highest use for a couple cats would be to make a pair of fuzzy slippers. I now had a cat and thought, "Gee, if I had two of her I could make a pair of slippers, *ha ha ha.*" Meet "Slipper," ship's cat. She has been a crew member and my sailing companion ever since. Cats do indeed have personality.

Rounding out *Pato's* crew is "the mask." The mask is a unique piece of wood that once belonged to Hippie Doug. It has the appearance of a one-eyed screaming pirate, or something like that. It had been a fixture on the dashboard of every vehicle he owned since he found it (or it found him) on a beach somewhere. When Doug passed on, I asked his brother if he knew what had become of it. I was deeply touched when he offered it to me. It has now sailed many thousands of miles on *Laughing Wind* and *Pato Feo*. For me it is a daily reminder of the values that Doug espoused.

My first year with *Pato* I adjusted from life in a sixteen-hundred square foot home to a tiny little boat, and took many short cruises and day sails on the familiar waters of Puget Sound. It is an amazing thing to find out just how little stuff you really need. In the words of Robin Lee Graham in the book *Dove*, "The Sea has taught me not how much I need, but how little."

Chapter Four

Springtime, when earth awakens. For me, the spring of 2006 also promised a reawakening, or perhaps more accurately, a rebirth; a new beginning. Years of dreaming, months of planning and preparation were soon to come to fruition.

My marriage of twenty-eight years had ended on the winter solstice, my divorce from Peewee having become final on December 21.

I was seeing a bright new future beyond the horizon. I hoped to finally live my life as I saw fit.

Peewee was seeing the world she knew fall apart. For her, our life together had been relatively comfortable. She hadn't wanted the divorce.

Peewee had long maintained a good career. She'd been very good at what she did and was well respected by her peers. The stress of the divorce took a huge toll on her, and her work began to suffer. She lost her job ... and another. She turned to the bottle. She continued to cling to the hope that we would reunite, that I'd come to my senses and everything would get back to normal. Was this just another in my long string of mid-life crises, she wondered? I tried to be as fair and supportive as possible throughout the painful process. As Peewee struggled to find her way, I tried to help her in any way I could. I was unable to simply turn my back on her. We had spent thirty years together, our entire adult lives, and raised two wonderful children. The more helpful and supportive I was the more she seemed to feel the loss. In hindsight, perhaps it would have been easier on her if I'd been a total asshole; sometimes you have to be "cruel to be kind".

My so-called career of thirty years had also been left behind, hopefully forever. (I've learned to "never say never.") After the bloodsuckers (lawyers) got their share, the proceeds from the sale of our family home left me with enough to live on while I decided what to do with my life.

Friends like Daniel, Hippie Doug, and Yvonne had shown me how you can live on very little and still have a happy, rewarding and fulfilling life. With my newfound lifestyle as a liveaboard, my living expenses were minimal. I would no longer be an active participant in the rat race.

I had no desire to have a six-thousand square foot house with a three-car garage, in a gated community with a name including "pond," "meadow," "forest," "brook," "glen," "wood" or "shore," to make you imagine a beautiful pastoral setting when all traces of such beauty have been comprehensively and systematically obliterated. Nor did I want an F-350 super-ultra-mega-duty 4x4 Phase II double mega-turbo grocery-getter pickup, a Corvette, a Lexus, his and hers Harley-Davidsons with handlebar streamers and a Barbie basket, an RV, assorted ORVs, a ski boat, a few jet-skis, a timeshare condominium in Hawaii, etc., etc., etc. It seems that all of America is caught up in this mad need for more and more, bigger and bigger stuff. We want it now and we want a lot of it! "Now you too can have all this and more with no money down and low, low monthly payments of next-to-nothing forever with instant credit approval and a low interest rate of only XXX% per month APR compounded annually." In order to have all of this "stuff" you need a high-paying job with all the associated stress. You'll work long hours which will leave you no time to enjoy the toys you think you own. You'll need to be prepared to sit in the daily gridlock we call a commute alongside all the other rats in the race. I've learned that you don't own your stuff, it owns you!

As my impending divorce had drawn near, I'd begun to plan for my future. I had gotten a job as a relief deckhand on the *Charlie Wells*, the private ferry serving Herron Island. It was an opportunity to start a new career as a mariner. I hoped to gain the sea days and experience necessary to obtain my 100-ton master's license, which would allow me to serve as relief skipper of the *Charlie Wells*.

I was also planning a lengthy voyage, and experiencing some pangs of guilt. Maybe this was a time when I needed to be available for Jason and Nicole. They were twenty-one and nineteen years old, but they had seen their family structure crumble. They were sharing an apartment, which made my heart glad, knowing they were getting along well and able to comfort one another through a very difficult time. They acted strong, and I believe they were, yet, I had the ability to earn a decent income and help them financially with college plans. Should I or could I postpone my plans?

I searched my soul and came to realize that if I was to be there for the kids when they needed me, I first had to make myself whole. I needed time to lick my wounds. Time to heal. Time to live.

Welcome aboard! Allow me to take you on a tour of the sailing vessel *Pato Feo*, my accommodations, my transportation, and my recreation, all in one neat package.

Images and information in the following pages are excerpts from Coronado's very comprehensive owner's manual. *Pato's* manual was prepared before the era when computers and word processors became commonplace, so the text was produced using a typewriter. Remember those?

Those were also before the days of computer aided design (CAD) programs. The yacht was designed by William H. Tripp on a drafting table, with pencils, rulers, and slide rules. Copies of his original drawings are utilized throughout the manual, but it is amusing to note that there are actually a few original pencil drawings included. That's right, some of the manual is done in pencil!

Enjoy your tour!

Sail Plan

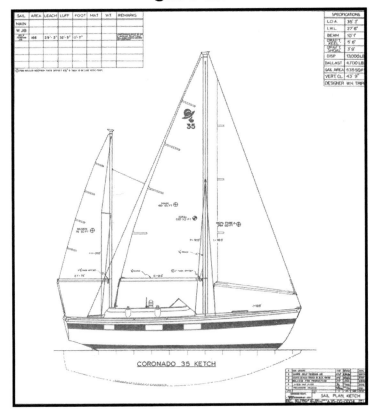

CORONADO 35 KETCH

This is the sail plan for the Coronado 35 ketch. A ketch can be recognized by having two masts, a main mast forward (the taller of the two masts) and a mizzen mast, aft. The Coronado 35 ketch design calls for a total sail area of 535 square feet: 192 feet for the main, 264 feet for the jib, and 79 feet for the mizzen.

Among cruisers I've met in my travels, the ketch is quite a popular rig. Among a ketch-rigged boat's advantages is that it can be balanced to sail itself by trimming or easing the mizzen sail. Although there is one more sail to handle than on a sloop (which has only a main mast), sails on a comparably-sized ketch are a little smaller and easier to handle. Many sailors have also found success in sailing a ketch in heavy air under jib and mizzen alone, although I have not personally had success with this configuration.

A ketch is similar in appearance to a yawl, but can be distinguished by the mizzen mast's location. On a ketch, the mizzen is stepped forward of the rudder post. On a yawl it is stepped aft, and often a yawl's boom extends well aft of the transom. A schooner also has two or more masts, but will have a main mast aft and a foremast forward.

Few would argue that a ketch under a full press of canvas is a beautiful sight!

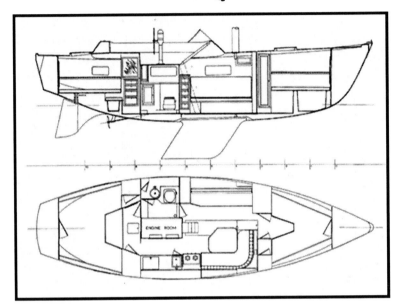

This is the cabin layout of *Pato Feo*.

At the bow is a chain locker. Just aft of the chain locker is the forward cabin with a V-berth, which will comfortably sleep two and includes a hanging locker (closet) to port and drawers to starboard. The door of the hanging locker doubles as a cabin door for privacy. Fuel and water tanks are concealed under the V-berth.

Moving aft, next is the cozy but not cramped saloon (not salon!). To port is a settee which will convert to upper and lower bunks to sleep two. A bank of house batteries is located under the settee and there is storage behind. To starboard is another settee and a table suitable for dining or reading charts.

Aft of the saloon are the head (to port) and the galley (to starboard), separated by the engine room. The head consists of a marine sanitation device (toilet), sink and shower. The galley has a three-burner propane range with oven, in addition to the sink and refrigerator. There is access to the engine from all four sides.

Next is the aft cabin, the feature that distinguishes the Coronado 35 from most sailing vessels. Large enough that I am able to use a full-size mattress, this cabin's size allows me to make up my bed using sheets and blankets rather than a sleeping bag (fart sack). To port are drawers, to starboard a hanging locker that also contains the refrigerator compressor and battery charger. Beneath the bunk are another set of batteries, the water heater, and the head's holding. At the stern is yet another locker, accessible through the aft cabin.

There are numerous storage compartments in the boat, although many are rather difficult to access. There is standing headroom throughout. The port-lights (windows) provide light and viewing even while seated. The cabin is nicely appointed with oiled teak and brass.

This humble boat has been my home for a number of years now: *mi casa del mar!*

Deck Layout

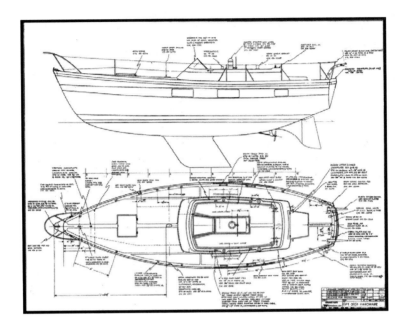

  This is the deck layout of the Coronado 35. Note that there is no raised cabin trunk, thus the port-lights (windows) are located in the topsides (the area between the waterline and the deck). The center cockpit design provides a spacious deck with lots of room to move about. Cockpit seating is quite high above the water, affording very good visibility in all directions. Helm and compass binnacle are in the cockpit's center. At its forward end is the companionway hatch. You descend to the cabin via seven steps on the companionway ladder. Located on the bow is the manual anchor windlass (not shown). On the stern are davits for raising and lowering a dinghy. Hatches located above the fore and aft cabins allow for ventilation, light, and emergency exits. It is a wonderful feeling to lie in my cozy bunk beneath an open hatch and watch stars twinkling overhead! The deck is resplendent, with just the right amount of brightwork (varnished wood), which is to say none!

Wiring Diagram

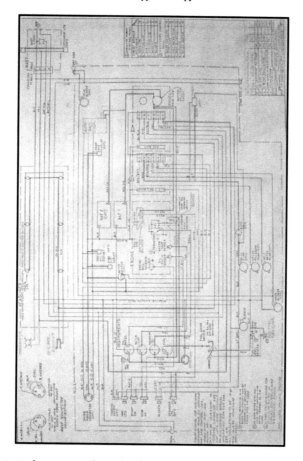

   This is the wiring diagram from my Coronado 35 owner's manual. In salt air, corrosion is a constant problem, and it is often necessary to effect repairs. The wiring diagram is very valuable, although it can be rather difficult to follow. Some portions of the diagram have been traced with colored pencils to correspond with the color coding of the wires themselves. Although I am no electromagician, I have learned that when working with electromagicity, the number one rule is: Don't let the smoke out of the electrical hose!

Bilge Pump Design

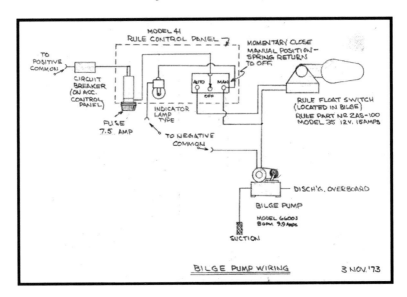

This page of the manual is an actual pencil drawing. The design was put to the test when *Pato* nearly sunk in her slip due to a broken fresh water hose!

Part Two
Cast off the lines that hold the past

And so the adventure began, sort of! I had planned a March 21 departure, to coincide with the vernal equinox, the first day of spring. My marriage had ended on the winter solstice, and I'd spent the winter regrouping. My planned departure date arrived, but I was embroiled in building a deck for my friend, and felt compelled to finish what I'd started, so I stayed on. Then, at the last minute I was called to work for a week on the *Charlie Wells*.

Saturday, April 1, 1300 hours Instead of heading north as planned, I laid a course south for Herron Island, cast off the lines and set off! The weather was pretty much what you'd expect for Western Washington in the spring, partly sunny with broken clouds, occasional showers, and flukey winds. On board with me was Ed, who had bought *Laughing Wind*, now *Teacher's Pet*. (His wife, Mary Jo, is a teacher.) Ed decided to accompany me as far as Gig Harbor. We made sail, moving out of Sinclair Inlet and through Rich Passage, then past Blake Island, and south down Colvos Passage, beating to weather in the southerly wind. I flew my 130 genoa for the first time and found that *Pato* was well balanced in up to twenty knots of wind, although she was a little overpowered, heeling up to thirty degrees.

As we neared Gig Harbor, the end of the throttle cable came loose. I repaired it while under way, and then discovered that the number two position on the master switch wasn't working. I was glad I had discovered these problems before I was in the wilds of Canada. We arrived at Gig Harbor, and by 2000 hours were tied up at the municipal dock, which offers 48 hours for free.

Gig Harbor had changed a lot since my youth. Having been raised nearby, my first job (circa 1970) had been at the grocery in downtown Gig Harbor. The harbor had an active fishing fleet then, many vessels having been purse seiners built at the Skansie boatyard in Gig Harbor. Those classic fishing boats of the past have been largely replaced by pleasure boats. and the quaint, working class town of my youth had become gentrified; a sanctuary for the rich and wannabes.

The next day, Ed caught a ride home. I repaired the master switch while moored at the dock, and then anchored in the heart of the harbor. I would spend a few days just hanging out in Gig Harbor and killing time. I didn't have to report for duty on the *Charlie Wells* until the tenth, so there was no need for haste.

Thursday, April 6 I waited in vain until early afternoon, hoping to see the wind build. At 1530 hours I caught the flood down through the Tacoma Narrows under power, then proceeded between Anderson and McNeil islands via Balch Passage. All of McNeil Island has been reserved as a state penitentiary, which has preserved it from development. Once past the penitentiary, McNeil Island is quite scenic. Unfortunately, it is off-limits to the public. I fetched Longbranch in Filucy Bay and set the hook at 1900 hours. Longbranch is a preferred anchorage of mine, a convenient stopover when traveling to and from Herron Island.

Friday, April 7, 0936 hours I weighed anchor and got under way for Herron Island. It was another beautiful spring day. Winds were variable northerlies five to fifteen knots. I made sail on a broad reach until I cleared Devil's Head, and then beat to weather up Case Inlet to Herron Island. I set the hook at the north end of the island at 1500 hours. Although this put me on a lee shore, I knew it to be a good holding ground and that the wind usually dies down at sunset. I would spend a couple of days seeing old friends and acquaintances I'd known when I had my cabin there.

Herron Island is about a mile long and accessible only to members and guests via their private ferry, the *Charlie Wells*. You'd expect it to be another playground for the rich, but although there are a few "McMansions," most homes on the island are quite humble, sheltering a mix of year-round residents and weekenders. Many lots remain undeveloped, some occupied by camping trailers. There are two community beaches, three parks, and a small boat dock and launch ramp. The many resident deer will eat right out of your hands. The roads are gravel and there is a fifteen mile an hour speed limit. On Herron, you get to know your neighbors and can always count on a friendly wave and smile. The island will always hold a special place in my heart.

My shift on the *Charlie Wells* would begin the afternoon of Monday, April 10. My duties would include handling the mooring lines, operating the ramp, loading and unloading vehicles, and serving as purser.

As I readied myself for work that Monday, it occurred to me that *Pato Feo* had become my accommodation, my transportation, and my recreation all in one neat package. I had just enjoyed sailing (recreation) to work (transportation) in my home (accommodation). Millions commuted in stop-and-go traffic from their cookie cutter homes in the suburbs and for entertainment(?) had their TVs. Many of them had incomes in six figures, whereas my income could hardly be counted in four figures! Would I trade my life for theirs? I think not!

The *Charlie Wells* was launched in 1989. She is sixty-five feet overall with a forty-eight foot beam. Her gross tonnage is ninety-nine tons, and she is approved for forty-nine passengers and twelve vehicles. With so many people driving vehicles the size of small houses, sometimes we're only able to fit eight or ten. The crossing takes about ten minutes. The ferry leaves the mainland on the hour and the island on the half-hour; back and forth, back and forth. You'd think it would get boring, but the ever-changing water and sky, and the play of light on the Olympic Mountains provide adequate stimulation.

With my duty on the ferry completed on Friday morning, I was free to get under way again. I would return to Port Orchard to complete my provisioning before finally heading out on my adventure. At 1400 hours, I weighed anchor and got under way.

Clarey, a friend I'd met on the island would accompany me as far as Longbranch. Winds were rather blustery, from five to twenty-five knots southerly. It made for rather interesting sailing! Good ol' *Pato* performed pretty well, although she did have a lot of weather-helm and I made a note to try tuning the rig for better balance. We fetched Filucy Bay at 1800 hours, where I dropped Clarey off at the dock in Longbranch, topped off the water tank then dropped the hook in the bay.

Saturday April 15, 1055 hours I made sail for Gig Harbor on the ebb. The weather was mostly sunny with southerly winds of five to fifteen knots, and sailing was great! In no time I had fetched Gig Harbor, but I was enjoying sailing so much that I decided to continue on up Colvos Passage. The current runs predominantly north in the passage and riding the last of the ebb gave me a real boost. It was slack water as I passed Blake Island and I was able to ride the first of the flood through Rich Passage and into Sinclair Inlet. I would lie at anchor close to the marina, as I had sublet my slip to Ed for *Teacher's Pet*. At 2000 hours I dropped the anchor under sail for the first time. It had been such a great day of sailing that I didn't want to spoil the tranquility of the moment by starting the motor.

I would spend a week in "Po-Dunk" doing last minute preparations and securing the last of my provisions. I changed oil and filters, topped off fuel and water tanks, and performed preventive maintenance where required. I took care to buy all of the charts and other publications I was likely to need, such as tide and current guides. I made sure to visit as many friends and family as possible. Soon, very soon I would depart on my adventure!

Chapter Six

Sunday, April 23rd Let the games begin! At last the day for my departure had arrived. I'd tied up at a vacant spot in the marina to say my farewells. Jason was unable to make it due to work, but Nicole was there to see me off. With tears in her eyes she said goodbye. As she was leaving, she turned to me and said, "Don't die!" I assured her that although what I was setting out to do was not without risk, I promised to be careful.

With that I cast off the lines. At 1350 hours I got under way beneath bright, sunny skies. It was a beautiful, warm spring day. A small flotilla consisting of Daniel and Lori on *Vientos de Cambio*, Ed and Mary Jo on *Teacher's Pet*, and Jim and Charlotte on *Twenty-One* would accompany me out of Port Orchard. Joining me aboard *Pato* was Yvonne and, of course, Slipper. Yvonne would sail with me for an hour or so and return to port with Daniel. We all made sail in a northerly wind of fifteen knots.

Our small fleet sailed northeast out of Sinclair Inlet. Shortly we reached the point where I would continue on my way up the west side of Bainbridge Island toward Agate Pass, while the others returned to port. On the VHF, Daniel and I discussed how we would transfer Yvonne from *Pato* to *Vientos*. Soon we had a plan. As I sailed on a port tack, Daniel would bring *Vientos* alongside under my lee and Yvonne would step across at our closest approach. With both boats heeling, my lee rail was nearly even with his weather rail due to the difference in our freeboard. When we were about six inches apart and making five or six knots, Yvonne stepped across. Daniel and I had known each other for about twenty-five years and logged many miles together under sail. I can think of no one else I would perform this maneuver with. We have the utmost confidence in each other's boat handling abilities. Don't try this at home, kids!

With that, we separated. As we drew apart I dropped my pants and flashed my traditional farewell salute to the fleet. Some traditions must never die! I knew I would not see my friends for several months and I wanted to leave them with a lasting memory. I had a nice sail up past Illahee State Park and into Manzanita Bay. At 1900 hours I tossed out the hook.

I'd travelled but a few short miles on that first day, but I'd finally escaped. As darkness fell on my first night out, the Suquamish tribe put on a spectacular fireworks show at their reservation across Agate Pass. It brought Peewee to mind; she had always taken a childlike delight in fireworks. My thoughts were with her as I turned in for the night. I hoped that she would soon find herself on the healing path.

I awoke to a sunny, warm morning and got under way at 0919 hours. Winds were calm as I motored up Agate Pass and under the Bainbridge Island Bridge, but by the time I reached President Point, the wind had built to ten knots northerly. I decided to shake the wrinkles out of those big, baggy white things that make *Pato* a sailing vessel. The wind built to twenty knots plus and I took two reefs in the main to reduce heeling. As soon as I was done, the wind eased.

When I went below to fix a bite of lunch, I found water on the cabin sole and the saloon's starboard settee. When *Pato* heeled hard in the stronger puffs, the galley sink had gone below water level. Water had backed up the drain, filled the sink and overflowed. Note to self: In the future, close thy seacocks before ye make sail, lest ye fowl thy cabin!

I doused the sails when the wind died and motored through the cut between the Quimper Peninsula and Indian Island. I anchored just off the wooden boat school at Port Hadlock at 1905 hours. It had been one of those days that make you wonder why you chose to have a sailboat, but as I prepared to call it a night I was treated to a spectacular sunset.

Tuesday, April 25 Another bright, sunny day greeted me as I arose. I had a leisurely morning and weighed anchor at 1130 hours. The wind was blowing ten knots southerly and I made sail on a broad reach. To port, I passed the historic town of Port Townsend, which had been a major port in the days of sail. I opted to pass by, having made it a port of call on many prior occasions, but I'd highly recommend it to anyone. The town is full of beautiful buildings carefully preserved or restored by skilled craftsmen who have made it their trade to save historic buildings. Of more interest to the yachtsman is the community of wooden boat aficionados to be found there. Their annual Wooden Boat Festival draws thousands of boaters and admirers. There is a large marina and boatyard where you are free to walk the docks and admire many beautifully restored, classic wooden boats and observe the many craftsmen plying their trades. Another fun event is Port Townsend's annual, zany Kinetic Sculpture Race, which pits human-powered contraptions against one another on a several mile long course on land and sea. Rube Goldberg lives!

Off Point Hudson, the wind eased to five knots. When I rounded Point Wilson and reached the Strait of Juan de Fuca, I encountered twenty to twenty-five knot westerlies and relatively rough water.

Plan "A" was to make for Stuart Island. I soon found that plan to be a bit ambitious as the current was not in my favor. Plan "B" was to turn back and make Sequim Bay. Plan "C," (what plan?) was to continue across the strait to Lopez Island in the San Juans under a double reefed main, the genoa and the mizzen.

Pato got a real workout as I sailed a beam reach. She was heeling hard and taking the seas on her port quarter. The heavy air caused excessive weather-helm, the seas constantly trying to make her round up. I stood at the wheel and wrestled with her. It was exhilarating! I was struck by the beauty and power of the wind and water. The deepest of blues stood in sharp contrast to white foam blown on the wind.

Eventually, I fetched Lopez Island and proceeded under sail into Aleck Bay. At 2000 hours I dropped anchor. It had been a tiring but exciting day.

Wednesday April 26 was overcast. At 1200 hours I set out for Stuart Island via Harrow Strait. Although the winds were only about five knots southerly, I sailed wing-n-wing under the main and genoa for a while. Daniel had loaned me his spinnaker pole for my journey, and I found that using it as a whisker pole and my vang as a preventer made sailing off the wind much easier. At 1850 hours I made my way into Reid Harbor on Stuart Island.

This had been the extremis of my first cruising adventure aboard *Pamplonica* just a few short years before. The island has two good harbors, Reid Harbor and Prevost Harbor, separated by an isthmus which is also a state park. At the far end of the island is the scenic

Turn Point lighthouse. The few roads are unpaved and there is no ferry service. Electricity is not provided nor is there community water or telephones. Provisions must be brought in by boat or by air; there are no supermarkets. There is a one-room schoolhouse on the grounds where the original school remains, now a museum. The new school is an interesting fan-shaped building constructed of logs and heated with wood. Visiting Stuart Island is like taking a trip back in time.

On Thursday, I took a lay-day. I rowed ashore, calling my usual command, "Stay *Pato*, stay! Good duck!" I enjoyed a pleasant walk among familiar sights while I awaited Daniel and Lori, who were flying up to visit in Daniel's Cessna one-fifty. We wished to see each other one more time before I disappeared over the edge of the earth.

For access to shore, on my davits I carried an eight-foot fiberglass dinghy equipped with oars. My dinghy had been included in the purchase of *Pato* and had the appearance of a refugee from a dumpster, but I found it better to carry a throw-away dinghy than a thousand dollar plus inflatable. This way I didn't have to worry about damaging it by dragging it across rocks, barnacles and oysters found on many beaches. Also, I'd once been caught in a following sea while towing a dinghy on a painter. It had constantly tried to surf up under the transom and I'd nearly had to cut the painter. If I found myself in such a situation again, I promised myself that I would not put *Pato* at risk to protect the dinghy. I would cut the painter or the davit lines, something I would be reluctant to do with a dinghy that cost thousands of dollars.

I was soon to make a discovery about Stuart Island. There are actually *two* small, private airports with grass strips on Stuart. I was only aware of one and Daniel was only aware of the other. I walked to the airport and waited … and waited. We were unable to make contact by cell phone due to poor signals and eventually, I gave up and walked back to the dock where I'd left my dinghy. The dinghy was not where I'd left it! Looking up the harbor, I saw Daniel and Lori out having a nice row. In my absence, my vacant boat lying in a peaceful harbor had been too much of a temptation. They knew they would not be disturbed because they had my dinghy. It was beginning to seem that *Pato* was becoming a playground for everyone's sexcapades but mine! Even Ed and Mary Jo had once snuck aboard at the marina and frolicked in my bunk. Something was seriously wrong with this picture! Together we went for a nice walk and too soon I had to see them off at the airport. At least now I knew where it was.

I spent the rest of the day gathering ingredients for my evening meal. In the woods I found some oyster mushrooms. On the beach I found a few oysters. My crab pot provided a couple of nice Dungeness crabs. With these in hand I had a wonderful meal provided by Mother Earth.

Friday, April 28 I arose to a clear sky and no wind, so it was under power that I proceeded up the southwest shore of Stuart Island. I cleared the lighthouse at Turn Point and made for Bedwell Harbor on South Pender Island where I intended to clear customs into Canada. In the distance Mount Baker was visible in all her grandeur.

When I reached the customs dock, it was deserted and I used the phone provided outside the office to contact a customs officer. It seemed that the office is only open during the peak boating season. It would not be open for a couple of days. I feared that I'd have to go to Sydney on Vancouver Island, which would have been a real inconvenience aboard a boat that cruises at five knots.

It was my lucky day though. It seems that a yacht club was having a rendezvous in Bedwell Harbor and had made arrangements to clear customs by phone. By coincidence, their rendezvous occurred the same day that I arrived in Canada. After a brief conversation, the officer gave me my clearance number and I was free to be on my way.

When travelling in a foriegn country, I find it beneficial to be multi lingual in dealing with customs officials, and fortunately, I am fluent in English, American, Australian, and Canadian, eh? I also hablo mierda del toro, Je parle la merde de taureau, and Ich spreche Stierscheiße. In other words, I speak bull shit!

Only five short days before, I'd said my farewells at my home port and I'd already left the U.S. behind. Perhaps I was trying to make up for lost time before the time was lost.

Chapter Seven

So I once again found myself in Canadian waters. I was in the Gulf Islands, so named because in the days of discovery the Strait of Georgia was thought to be a gulf. The error was eventually found and corrected, but the archipelago's name stuck. The Gulf Islands are essentially a continuation of the San Juan Islands, separated by Boundary Passage and Haro Strait and marked by a zigzag dotted line in the water as shown on the chart. Several times I've looked for this line in the water to no avail; apparently it's been erased. Five or six long, narrow islands form a barrier, protecting the rest of the group from the violent weather that regularly occurs in the Strait of Georgia. A number of passes breach this barrier. Like the San Juans, the Gulf Islands are quite scenic. Both are accessible to vehicles only by ferry, many of which ply these waters; there are no bridges. Due to the Gulf Islands' close proximity to the cities of Vancouver and Victoria as well as the U.S., they are popular with boaters.

Having cleared customs, I left Bedwell Harbor and headed up Swanson Channel past North Pender and Prevost Islands. I then passed south of Saltspring Island and made my way into Montague Harbor, located between Galiano Island and much smaller Parker Island, where I would spend my first night in Canada. I set the hook at 1725 hours, had dinner, and called it a day.

Montague Harbor is a port of call for the B.C. ferries. It's public dock, generally referred to as a "government dock" by the locals, allows easy access to shore. Government docks are easily identified by their distinctive red-painted railings. The village at Montague Harbor appeared to have many facilities needed by boaters, but I needed no provisions so chose not to go ashore.

During my voyage I would bypass many interesting towns and villages, places that might tempt me to spend what little money I had saved. For the most part I would only visit towns out of necessity, when in need of fuel, water, provisions, or perhaps a cheeseburger fix. On rare occasions I might actually crave human contact. It's not that I was antisocial. I didn't want to become a hermit; maybe a sea hobo would be more fitting.

Saturday, April 29 I awoke to overcast skies and drizzle. I got under way at 1000 hours and headed northwest up Trincomali Channel. The wind was northwesterly about five knots, but I shook 'em out (made sail) anyway as winds were expected to build and the weather supposed to fair.

As I was beating to weather, I was startled by a sound off *Pato's* port quarter. I turned to see a mother Orca and her calf about fifty feet away and paralleling my course! A short time later the rest of the pod – including several bulls, cows, and calves – came alongside. We would cross each other's paths on several occasions as I tacked back and forth in the narrow channel, and they remained in sight for a few hours. No matter how many times I encounter these wonderful creatures, it never fails to be a thrill.

Soon I had to make a choice whether to continue up Trincomali Channel or turn to port and follow Houstoun Passage. I chose to stay the course in Trincomali, as did my friends, the Orcas. At Hall Island I again reached a crossroad. I chose to follow the channel to port along the north-eastern shore of Thesis Island. When I reached the northern tip, I threaded my way between the Ragged Islets and their outlying reef and continued around Thesis to Telegraph Harbor, where I tossed out the hook at 1700 hours.

The stronger winds never did find their way into the Gulf Islands that day, and showers had continued throughout. That evening I went ashore for a stroll and met a man who'd crossed the Strait of Georgia from Vancouver that morning in his Zodiac. He had battled fifty knot winds and ten foot seas in his crossing. He asked if I'd care to buy his boat ... cheap! Long, narrow Galiano Island had done its job by effectively sheltering the Gulf Islands from the blow.

At this point in my journey I really didn't have an overall objective or course in mind. I merely wanted to see and experience nature before her remnants were destroyed. I also wanted to see whether all of humanity was caught up in the madness and greed that I saw consuming America.

I had two small-scale nautical charts that covered the area from Olympia, Washington to Queen Charlotte Strait, at Vancouver Island's north end. Due to their small scale they were of little use in navigation, but I put them to use in planning and recording my travel. Each day I would locate the place I'd anchored and place a dot followed by the date. I would then connect the dots and draw an arrow on the line to indicate my direction of travel. This served me well, but some portions of the charts became very cluttered in areas I tended to frequent. I began to seek out areas on the charts which were unmarked. Often I would venture into an area simply because I'd not yet drawn any lines on that part of the chart.

Ever since I'd begun planning my adventure, the idea of circumnavigating Vancouver Island had been high on my list of possibilities. The portions of my charts covering the island's west coast were not marked beyond Barkley Sound. Vancouver Island's western, or "outside," shore is exposed to the Pacific Ocean, which makes sailing the outside very different than sailing the water off its eastern, or "inside," shore. Most cruisers choose to go up the inside and down the outside in order to take advantage of prevailing winds and currents. I had hoped to go the unconventional route – up the outside – because I'm, well, unconventional and perhaps more than a little contrary. Also, I've long preferred going to weather (sailing upwind) rather than sailing off the wind (downwind), and *Pato* can be balanced by sail trim to sail herself very well on the wind, requiring much less concentration than when sailing her off the wind. Also, I'd hoped to reach the outside during the annual Gray Whale migration, which brings them into the waters off Vancouver Island's western shore in early spring.

When listening to Environment Canada's weather reports on the VHF, I'd been paying particular attention to the part pertaining to west coast Vancouver Island, south. Unfortunately, most mornings the forecast was for gale warnings. I'd now reached the point in my journey at which I had to make my decision, take a risk or play it safe. Nicole's parting words; "don't die" came to mind. I opted to play it safe. Inside it would be.

Chapter Eight

With my decision to stay inside, it was time to choose a direction to wander. On my earlier voyage in *Laughing Wind*, I'd travelled up the Gulf Islands, through Dodd Narrows and past Nanaimo, then across the Strait of Georgia to Pender Harbor. Having already traversed this area, I looked for alternatives.

In reviewing my charts, I discovered that Howe Sound remained completely unmarked. Due to its proximity to the metropolis of Vancouver I was reluctant to venture there, fearing it would be like the area surrounding Seattle, with a population in the millions. Daniel and I had once ventured to the Broken Group for no other reason than having possessed the chart. I had a chart of Howe Sound in my possession, so I had no choice but to go there.

Sunday, April 30 With my decision made, I got under way at 0900 hours. I proceeded under power, following a course down and around Kuper and Tent Islands while giving Sandstone Rocks a wide berth. I then weaved my way through Norway, Hall and Reid Islands and made my way into Portlier Pass right at the tail of ebb tide. I was only able to make about two knots under power against the current.

Winds of up to twenty-five knots were forecast for the Strait of Georgia, so while "Otto" (my auto-pilot) manned the helm I made sail in readiness for the impending blow. When I was finally able to fight my way through the pass and into the Strait, I was greeted by a flat calm; not so much as a breath of wind. The water was like a mirror. So much for a blow! I must have looked rather foolish having all of my sails aloft. At least they provided shade from the bright sun.

As I neared Howe Sound, having crossed the Strait, I caught a ride on the inflow winds that occur in the sound. I'd noticed that weather reports often reported an inflow followed by an outflow, sometimes more than once a day, and indeed, the sound tends to "breathe" as the temperature rises and falls over the water and the surrounding tall mountains. Such fluctuations can make for challenging sailing. I talked to another sailor who told me he once flew a spinnaker all the way around Bowen Island, as the wind had shifted throughout the day. At least I hadn't gone to the trouble of making sail for naught.

I sailed a broad reach up Collingwood Channel to the west of Bowen Island, then continued around the north end and sailed a close reach down Queen Charlotte Channel to Mannion Bay. I anchored at 1930 hours, choosing a spot outside the fairway leading to Mannion Bay's government dock. I was still well provisioned, so there was no need to go ashore.

I had not been sure what to expect in Howe Sound. Would there be wall-to-wall houses? An industrial area? Would its hillsides be denuded of trees? I was totally unprepared for what I found. It was magnificent! There were beautiful wooded islands, sparsely populated apart from a few small villages. Majestic mountains rose from the sea, snow still clinging to their peaks. Further down their slopes, numerous waterfalls cascaded to the sea. Workers commuted in small runabouts. Ferries shuttled to and fro. What a treat it was to find nature's beauty thriving a few short miles from bustling Vancouver !

Monday, May 1, 0930 hours I set out to see more of the sound. I motored out of Mannion Bay, rounded up into the wind, and made sail. I then fell off and pointed the bow north toward the head of Howe Sound. It would be a day to simply indulge in the joy of sailing and enjoying scenery.

Winds were expected to be twenty to twenty-five knots, so I opted to fly my self-tending working jib. I'd been having a problem with foot flutter on the jib (if I was sailing in heavy air it sounded like a helicopter was landing on the foredeck), and I wanted to try some changes in trim to alleviate the problem. My sails were very old, so I didn't expect any miracles, but I did find some success in minimizing the problem.

I sailed a series of broad reaches as I rode the inflow winds against the ebb tide. The wind carried me up Montagu Channel and into Squamish Harbor, where I found one of a few small industrial complexes located along the sound.

Having reached the end of Howe Sound, I reversed course, rounded up into the wind, and began beating to weather, close-hauled. As expected, the inflow winds were about twenty-five knots.

The relative calm and silence of sailing downwind quickly vanished, the wind was roaring in the rigging. By then the tide had turned, so I was bucking the flood. Sailing was exhilarating! *Pato* took it all in stride.

I passed north of Anvil Island and down Ramillies Channel, then made my way around the southern tip of Gambier Island at Hope Point. There I had three small bays to choose from for anchorages: Port Graves, Center Bay and West Bay. First in line was Port Graves. I went in and saw no reason to look further.

I chose an anchorage near the government dock, where I dropped the hook at 1936 hours. I was a little concerned that the inflow winds might funnel into these south-facing bays, so I let out a generous scope.

My ground tackle consists of a thirty-five pound CQR anchor with a hundred feet of five-sixteenth inch chain and two hundred feet of five-eighth inch, three-strand nylon rope. I have marked the anchor rode at thirty foot intervals with one zip-tie at thirty feet, two at sixty feet and so on. I also carry a Danforth anchor and spare rode in reserve, as well as three hundred feet of polypropylene line on a hose reel for stern-tying.

When preparing to anchor, I approach shore and read my depth sounder to get a feel for the slope of the bottom. (One doesn't want to swing in the night and find they've gone aground.) I also check my GPS for how high the water is at that point in the tide, and how much it will rise or fall in the night. With that I find my spot, read the depth under the keel, and add ten feet (six for my draft and four to the bow roller). Using that number I calculate my scope based on the highest water I can expect for that night. In light air or very sheltered anchorages I might have a scope of only 3:1 or perhaps 5:1, if there is room. In less sheltered anchorages or if I expect a blow, I try for a 5:1 minimum. In *Chapman's Piloting and Seamanship*, a sort of "boater's bible, they recommend a scope of 7:1 to 10:1. Mr. Chapman , I defy you to find many anchorages where this is practical. Next I drop anchor and back down on it, usually toward shore, while observing my speed on the GPS. When the anchor brings the boat to a stop, the anchor is set. Periodically, I check to be sure the anchor is not dragging, and call it good. The process sounds complicated, but in practice it is quite simple. I have always slept well, knowing that I am going to wake up in the same place I started.

On this voyage, the daily ritual of weighing anchor proved to be a great workout. I would pull the rode hand-over-hand until I reached the point where I needed to break the anchor out, and then I would use my manual windlass to break it free. I would then bring it home by hand, making sure to use my legs and not my back.

Overnight the wind piped up to over twenty knots and when I arose in the morning, I discovered one of my folding deck chairs had abandoned ship. Although I scanned the shoreline for it with my binoculars, it was not to be found. The good news was that my anchor had done its job admirably.

It had been a few days since I'd set foot on solid ground, so I grabbed my walking stick, lowered my dinghy, and rowed to the nearby government dock. At the head of the dock is Camp Artaban, which appeared to be a Christian youth camp. A sign pointed to a trail leading to Lost Lake. I made my way along the well-marked trail that led past a small group of modest vacation homes and into the deep woods. Along the way I paused to stand inside a burned-out cedar stump. By counting the number of growth rings per inch in a part where they could be seen, I surmised that the tree had probably been over a thousand years old when it died. It was hard to imagine that the forest had once been filled with such giants.

In places, there remained portions of an old skid road made of cedar logs. A hundred years ago, lumberjacks regularly sent freshly-felled timber skidding along the surface of those logs to the waterfront, where the timber was made into rafts and towed to the hungry mills. When I finally made my way to Lost Lake, it was from one of these skid road logs that I plunged naked into the lake. To say that it was refreshing would be a gross understatement. It was cold!!! I shot back out of the lake and allowed the warm sun to dry my skin before I dressed and headed back down the trail. It had been an invigorating hike. I ate a hearty dinner and turned in, satisfied with the day and looking forward to the morning, when I would embark on the next leg of my journey.

Chapter Nine

Wednesday, May 3 I awoke to clear, sunny skies and prepared to get under way. Howe Sound had been a delightful surprise. I'd seen enough to realize that it warranted further exploration, but I would save that for the future. Because of its relative proximity to my home waters, I knew that I could return when I had a little time to spend. I looked at it as banking future adventures. In a high-speed power boat one could explore the entire Puget Sound in a matter of days. By exploring the region at a slow pace, I could savor the experience over several years. (Although there are now few areas I've yet to see, my "bank account" is not yet empty.)

Having made my "bank deposit," I weighed anchor at 1000 hours and motored out of Port Graves. At the mouth of the harbor, I made sail and began beating my way out of Howe Sound against the twenty-five knot inflow. At Keats Island, I turned to follow Barfleur Passage out to the Strait of Georgia. When I reached the strait, the winds eased to fifteen knots northwesterly, and I continued on my way sailing a series of close reaches.

One of the wonderful things about sailing is that some days it can be relaxing, others exciting, still others terrifying, but rarely is it boring. Some days you and your boat get on well and are in sync with one another; other days you may be at odds. Perhaps this is why most boats are named after women, as they too can be fickle. For *Pato*, a breeze of fifteen to twenty knots is perfect, but there are days when even under perfect conditions I find myself constantly trimming or easing the sheets and working the helm while struggling to find a balance. Some days I curse like a sailor because a halyard catches in the shrouds, or I get a riding turn on a winch, or a batten hangs up in the lazy-jacks. Of course, there is always the possibility that I am the one being fickle.

This was a day when *Pato* and I were in tune with one another. On the wind she was so well-balanced that I rarely had to touch the helm or a sheet, which allowed me ample time to reflect on life as nature worked it's magic on my fractured spirit.

When the wind dropped to ten knots, I cranked up the "iron oars" (the engine). Although ten knots is still adequate for nice sailing, I had too many miles to go before the next possible anchorage. So it was under power that I proceeded past Sechelt, Merry Island and Halfmoon Bay. There I followed Welcome Passage, which separates South Thormanby Island from the Sechelt Peninsula. The hour was growing late; it was time to find a place to hunker down for the night. I nosed into Smuggler Cove, home to one of British Columbia's many marine parks, but all the good anchorage spots were taken. I continued to nearby Secret Cove and anchored for the night.

Thursday, May 4 I rowed around the harbor for a while, stopping at one of the marinas to walk the docks and stretch my legs while admiring other boats. I never seem to tire of looking at them. I had a nice visit with Reg aboard his sixty-five foot ketch, *Pacific Wanderer*. She was a beautiful boat, inside and out, and her captain was a gracious host.

Refreshed by my row and stroll, I weighed anchor and made my way to the dock for fuel and water. I had switched to *Pato's* reserve tank only the day before, so I knew I had plenty of fuel on board, but I also knew that it is advisable to get fuel when and where you can when cruising in these waters. In some places water is more precious than fuel, and not always particularly palatable. When Daniel and I had last visited Pender Harbor, we had gone for a swim in the lake from which the village gets its water. The water had been the color of weak ice-tea, although it had tasted fine. When travelling in Canada, I tend to be very frugal with my water consumption.

Having topped off the tanks, I cast off the lines at 1430 hours and laid a course for Pender Harbor. It was another sunny and warm spring day, but there was no wind, so I proceeded under power. My destination was but a few short miles away, so it was not long before I arrived. I dropped the anchor at 1652 hours in Wellbourne Cove, near the government dock.

The last time I'd visited Pender Harbor, I had very much enjoyed the village. There you will find a couple of stores, several eateries and watering holes, laundry facilities, and a liquor store for those who are so inclined, as I used to be. Beer, spirits, and tobacco are very expensive in Canada. On my previous voyage through these waters, I'd had to stop every few days to buy beer and ice. It had been like having a leash around my neck. No longer being a slave to my drinking habit (addiction?) gave me a newfound sense of freedom. Alas, tobacco for my pipe was very difficult to find, and cost about triple what I was accustomed to paying in the U.S. When next I travel this way, I will have to consider giving up smoking or stocking up on tobacco before entering Canada.

I decided to stay a few days in Pender Harbor, the first town I had visited since I'd left Port Orchard nearly two weeks before. I needed to replenish my perishable provisions and do some laundry, and I was ready for a little human contact. I also really needed a "gut bomb" (hamburger). I found a great little burger stand where I was able to satiate my craving and discover an interesting Canadian custom. I was asked whether I would like gravy with my french-fries. As they say, "when in Rome, do as the Romans," so I gave it a try. It was interesting, but I think I'll stick to tartar sauce for my fries. (It's a Washingtonian thing.)

On Friday I went shopping for provisions and did my laundry. The only laundry facility I could find was at the far end of Garden Bay in an RV park, where they had a couple of beat-up, coin-operated washers and dryers. While my clothes were drying, I wandered next door to the local pub and found out that they had live music on Saturday nights. I decided it might be fun to take in the local nightlife. I spent the day aboard *Pato*, reading and stuff, and that evening I rowed over to the pub. The music was nice and the food good. I struck up a conversation with a very attractive local gal. We had a nice visit, but it made me acutely aware of the fact that I had little, if any, experience that might help me land a date. Perhaps it was pointless since I would soon be on my way. Nonetheless, I had a great time and was glad for the experience.

Sunday, I didn't have anything in particular that needed doing other than getting some exercise. I could have set sail, but I just didn't feel compelled to move on. Not having a rigid timeframe allowed me the freedom to go with my feelings. Some days you just need to stand down, and this was one of those days.

You may have by now realized that this book is of little use as a cruise guide. If you wish to find the best gourmet restaurants, entertainment, museums, or where to find the best gift and souvenir shops, you'd best look elsewhere. If you are looking for suggested routes and waypoints or anchorages, you'll not find them here. There are countless books already in print in which you can find this type of information. There are also many publications provided by official government agencies which should be considered mandatory when embarking on a voyage of this nature. This is one man's story; my story of how I came to find a new way of life.

Chapter Ten

I'd left home only two weeks before, but I was already forming a daily routine. Each morning when my eyes slammed open, I'd start a pot of coffee to enjoy in my bunk while I read. Since becoming a liveaboard, I'd broken my addiction to TV and become a prodigious reader who sought out book exchanges along the way. Unfortunately, most exchanges are filled with romance novels. At one point, I became so desperate for something new to read that, yes, I did read one! Having finished my coffee and read a few chapters, I would breakfast while I listened to the weather report on the VHF. Then I would review my charts and plot a course for the day.

I always tried to pick an objective that I could reach before nightfall, preferring not to enter an unfamiliar cove in the dark. With destination in mind, I would check the tides and currents. If navigation was going to be a bit tricky, involving a lot of twists and turns, I might set up a number of waypoints and enter a route in my GPS. I'd opted to use my trusty handheld GPS and paper charts on this trip. I was reluctant to rely too heavily on electronics, although I had added an autopilot which I used extensively when under power.

Having decided on my route, or at least a general direction, I would weigh anchor and head for my destination, though seldom by the most direct route. On a voyage like this, it is the journey that matters, not the destination. If there was sufficient wind I would sail, if not I would motor. While under way, I might have a light lunch or at least a snack. When I arrived at my destination, I'd drop the anchor. If there was enough daylight remaining and the shore looked inviting, I might row ashore and explore the beach or the forest. Later I would enjoy a hearty dinner and do "galley wench detail" (KP for you land lubbers). I would then enjoy the last hours of daylight out on deck and watch the sunset. I might read a bit in my bunk before I turned in for the night.

Monday, May 8, 0800 hours I got under way and headed out of Pender Harbor. My plan was to sail around Nelson and Hardy

Islands via Malaspina Strait and Jervis Inlet before making my way into Hotham Sound. I had passed the mouth of the sound before, on a previous voyage, and had thought it quite beautiful but hadn't had time to explore it. Thus, that part of my chart had remained unmarked. Hotham Sound, like Howe Sound, is not a destination one hears talked about by many cruisers. This gave me reason enough to have a closer look.

The forecast was for northwesterly winds of ten to fifteen knots. Anticipating moderate winds, I hanked on the genoa and prepared to hoist a full press of canvas. When I reached Malaspina Strait at the mouth of the harbor, I was greeted by wind of twenty-five knots. I made the decision to switch back to the working jib and fly the main with two reefs. I also decided to try an experiment. I would try sailing under the jib and a double reefed main alone, abandoning the mizzen. I was convinced that this sail plan would work. After all, the Coronado 35 was available in both ketch and sloop versions, and the main masts are stepped in the same place. I would try to sail *Pato* as a sloop.

My experiment did not pan out. It induced a large amount of lee helm, and I was unable to make good headway when going to weather. When I raised the mizzen sail, the boat was better balanced but overpowered.

Others have told me that one of the ketch rig's advantages is the ability to balance the boat by flying only the jib and mizzen, without the main. With this in mind, I handed the main and tried to beat to weather under this sail configuration. I was unable to make good headway.

With growing frustration, I chose to retreat to Agamemnon Channel and pass around the other side of Nelson Island. Nelson sheltered the narrow channel from the blow and I found little wind, so I motor-sailed up the channel. Leaving Agamemnon Channel behind, I rounded Captain Island and crossed Jervis Inlet, where I found a nice westerly breeze of ten to twelve knots. I sailed a beam reach with all sails aloft to the head of Hotham Sound. There I reversed course and sailed back to have a closer look at the spectacular waterfall that cascades from Freil Lake into the sound, from a height of perhaps two thousand feet. It is truly a breathtaking sight.

Having had enough fun for one day, I ducked in behind the nearby Harmony Islands to seek shelter for the night. This small group of islands comprise yet another of British Columbia's marine parks. I found a small cove in which to anchor, but because the water was quite deep, found it necessary to rig a stern line to a tree on shore.

For those of you not familiar with this practice, I will try to briefly explain the procedure and the reason it is sometimes necessary. When you wish to anchor in a very tight space (such as a small cove or crowded anchorage) with deep water not far from shore, you are faced with a dilemma. If you let out little scope on your anchor rode, you may swing in a small circle but run the risk of dragging anchor. If you let out adequate scope, you may swing in a large enough circle to find yourself aground or fouling another boat's rode. By stern tying, you are able to let out adequate scope but prevent the boat from swinging. You are basically mooring your boat between your anchor and a fixed point on shore. Another option would be to rig a stern anchor to accomplish the same thing.

I start by sounding the bottom to get a feel for its shape and depth. Once I have found the best spot, I drop my bow anchor and back down on it toward the point on shore where I plan to rig my stern line. With the bow anchor set, I deploy my dinghy and head ashore, pulling my polypropylene line off the hose reel I have fixed to *Pato*'s stern. I use poly line due to its low cost, high visibility, and buoyancy. When I reach shore, I take a turn around a tree or rock and return to the boat with the bitter end, which I make fast to a cleat. I then take up on the standing part of the line and make a bight fast to another cleat. Next I adjust the scope on the anchor rode and the stern line to position the boat where desired. Finally, I sit and watch to be sure the anchor is holding.

Although it is not a difficult procedure, I always feel some trepidation when I leave my boat unattended to deploy the stern line. It would be less stressful to accomplish this task if you had a crew member standing by in case the boat decided to wander from its spot. Slipper is of no use in this matter.

On this particular night, while I was below fixing some dinner, I looked out the starboard port light and was startled to see that the rocks looked very close. I dashed on deck to find that the wind had shifted and my anchor was dragging on the rocky bottom. I quickly repeated the entire anchoring procedure. Oh well, practice makes perfect!

With dinner over and *Pato* now properly secured, I set out by dinghy to explore the Harmony Islands. I found the shore covered with oysters – so plentiful I could pick and choose any size I wanted. To eat raw on the half shell, I picked small bite-size ones. To pan fry, I chose slightly larger ones. I now had fresh seafood to enhance my diet. I had hoped to go for a walk, but the rugged terrain made this impractical. The thick moss that covers these rocky islands is very delicate; one misstep could cause much harm to the growth. While my impact alone might be of little consequence, mine combined with numerous other boaters could soon leave these islands bare. I respectfully chose to return to my dinghy and continue my exploration afloat.

Having gotten a little exercise, I returned to *Pato* and settled in for the night. It had been an exhausting day and I needed plenty of rest so I could get an early start. In the morning I would return to familiar waters; my objective the fabled Princess Louisa Inlet.

Chapter Eleven

Tuesday, May 9 I rose to a beautiful, sunny day. My destination for the day was beautiful Princess Louisa Inlet. I weighed anchor and got under way at 0750 hours in order to reach Malibu Rapids before high slack water at 1625 hours. With some thirty-five miles to make, at my cruising speed of five knots I would need about seven hours to get there. Malibu Rapids is a short, narrow, twisting channel separating Princess Louisa from Queens Reach. Its current is something to be reckoned with. Even powerful motor yachts must wait for slack water, lest they careen out of control in its swirling eddies. Recently a brand new mega-yacht had found itself high and dry on the rocks when its helmsman foolishly tried to power through.

I proceeded under power into Jervis Inlet and headed up into the reaches. Prince of Wales Reach, Princess Royal Reach, and Queens Reach comprise a long zigzag fjord that cuts into the coast of mainland British Columbia. There are very few signs of human activity apart from a few logging camps, some of which are abandoned. The scenery is breathtaking. Jagged granite mountains spring from the water to touch the sky. Vertical cliffs thousands of feet tall rise directly from waters some two to three hundred fathoms deep.

Leaving Hothom Sound behind, I rounded Foley Head and followed the shoreline through Dark Cove and Goliath Bay. I wanted to check for anchorages in Jervis Inlet. Once you head up the reaches, you are either fully committed to continuing on to your objective or to a complete retreat, as there are almost no satisfactory anchorages. I made a mental note of the area's possible shelters (there were a couple), in case I should need them in the future. With that I continued on my way.

Rounding Saumarez Bluff I entered Prince of Wales Reach. As I passed Vancouver Bay the wind rose to south-easterly fifteen knots, so I made sail and flew wing-n-wing up the reach. Sailing was pleasant, but a few short   miles later the wind died as I turned into Princess Royal Reach. Reluctantly, I handed the sails and continued under power. While Otto manned the helm, I kicked back and enjoyed the panorama.

For the first time on this voyage I stripped naked and sunbathed, enjoying the warm spring sun on my skin. This would become something I would do on a regular basis. It was a way to feel at one with nature.

When I rounded Patrick Point I entered Queens Reach, the last leg leading to Malibu Rapids and the wonders of Princess Louisa Inlet. I had made good time and would need to hover for a while to await slack water.

While I waited, I noticed another boat also waiting for the turn of the tide. She was *Talisman*, a Pearson 42 ketch out of Oregon. I motored over to say hi. Dean and Dianne had sold their log home, bought *Talisman*, and sailed forth on their way to points unknown. Their tentative plan was to travel up the inside of Vancouver Island then down the outside before continuing on to the Sea of Cortes. They had no particular timeframe in mind, nor any particular route.

To say that Dean was an avid fisherman would be a gross understatement. He made it a point to fish a little every day and rarely came up empty-handed. They invited me to dine with them that evening aboard *Talisman*. Dianne would be preparing her galley specialty: cioppino prepared with seafood Dean had caught. I gratefully accepted their invitation and agreed to join them aboard when we reached Chatterbox Falls at the head of the inlet.

When the tide turned, we continued on our way through Malibu Rapids. From the outside, the rapids have the appearance of a swift flowing river; in fact early explorers had mistaken it for one and its wonders had remained secret for some time. To port we passed Camp Malibu, a Christian youth camp. It appears to be quite a complex, with many buildings. A colorful array of bathing towels adorned the hand rail of one of the larger buildings. We exchanged friendly waves with the campers as we threaded our way through the passage. Leaving the rapids behind, we were then in spectacular Princess Louisa Inlet. The inlet is about three miles in length and a quarter mile in width. Along its shores are many vertical cliffs rising directly from the water. Several small waterfalls cascade from the cliffs.

Midway up the inlet you will pass Hamilton Island on your port side. When you reach the end of the inlet, you will find the crown jewel of Princess Louisa, Chatterbox Falls. The falls are fed by Loquilts Creek, which threads its way down the face of a massive granite mountain. It is interesting to look for images in the rock's face, as you might look for images in the clouds. There is a public dock located near the base of the falls, as well as a unique picnic shelter built of logs. There is no charge for use of the dock, as specified in the will of "Mack" MacDonald, who donated the falls and the surrounding land to the province of British Columbia. Mack had been a world traveler who, upon seeing the falls, had professed it to be the most beautiful place in the world. He had bought the land surrounding the falls and built a beautiful lodge, which he made his home. The lodge had burned to the ground long ago in a tragic fire, but Mack's legend is alive. Aboard nearly every yacht that visits Princess Louisa you will find a copy of *Mack and the Princess*, which tells Mack's story.

When I reached the end of the inlet, I was pleased to see that there was plenty of space available at the dock, a benefit of having arrived early in the boating season. I chose to moor there rather than anchor out. This would be the first time I would stay at a dock since I'd left Port Orchard.

That evening I joined Dean and Dianne aboard *Talisman* for dinner. Dianne's cioppino was truly delicious. It consisted of salmon, ling cod, halibut, rockfish, crab, clams, and mussels. To this I contributed some of the oysters I had gathered. Although I pride myself on my cooking ability, I must say that my culinary expertise pales in comparison. We had a delightful evening together.

In the morning, I set out to take a hike. The area has steep terrain with few trails, and where the trails lead up along the falls, care must be taken. The rocks become very slick with moss and algae, and many people have fallen to their death by not showing due respect. A sign at the base of the falls serves as a reminder by listing the names of those who have met their demise in this manner.

One trail leads to the ruins of an old trapper's cabin, high up on one of the mountains that surround the inlet. With my trusty walking stick in hand, I set out for the cabin. I followed the relatively well-marked trail until I reached a spot where a landslide had obliterated it. It is very steep in places and at times I found myself climbing up rocks or clinging to tree roots. Eventually I found my way to the ruins of the cabin. It was merely rubble, but the setting justified the effort it took to reach it.

The cabin had been built next to yet another beautiful waterfall. The site overlooks Princess Louisa from high above, and the view is simply breathtaking. I wondered what had possessed the trapper to make his home here? To my mind, this was not a likely place to find beavers, otters, or mink; nor would it have been a convenient place from which to transport or trade pelts. Perhaps the lone trapper had been struck by the grandeur and serenity of the site. One can only guess his motives.

I would spend a few days at Chatterbox Falls. I gathered a few succulent mussels and searched in vain for mushrooms. One evening we got a little rain and I joined some folks in building a fire in the MacDonald Memorial Lodge, a round, open-air picnic shelter constructed of large logs, with a centrally located fire pit. It was pleasant to visit with others while enjoying the crackle of a blazing fire.

Other yachts came and went. Soon there were four ketch-rigged yachts at the dock. It's a popular rig among the cruising set, and we were unanimous in our praise of its virtues.

Among the growing fleet at the dock, I alone was traveling solo. On this voyage, as well as my previous journeys, I'd grown accustomed to sailing singlehanded and had come to enjoy my own company. There are advantages to travelling and living alone. It is not necessary to discuss plans with another. You are free to come and go when and where you wish. Do as you will. Eat what you like. Fart, belch and scratch to your heart's content. You don't have to endure someone else's bitching and whining when the weather takes a turn for the worse or things go awry. It is difficult enough sharing your life with another while living ashore, much less in the cramped space of a boat.

On the other hand, you have no one with whom to share your joys and sorrows; you laugh and cry alone. At times, the refuge of your bunk can seem a cold, empty place. No one comforts you when you are troubled. You have no one with whom to share the special moments and memories. Shared memories seem more vivid.

At times I'd thought that the cruising lifestyle was for men only. Where could one ever hope to find a woman who would be able to live as I was? Many women would be repulsed at the notion of not bathing every day. How could they hope to exist without a hairdryer and all of the other modern conveniences? At the dock were not one but several couples who were cruising together. What was the key to their success? It was apparent from their manner and stories that these women did not simply endure but in fact loved the cruising life. They were an integral part of their crews.

These couples seemed to understand and appreciate how I was trying to live my life. They had what I had and so much more. They had that special person with whom they shared their life and their love.

My mind drifted back to Peewee. Why had I not been able to make her understand how I wanted to live? Many times I'd tried to convince her that there were simpler ways. At times I'd wanted to move out to the country and learn to farm. Later I'd wanted to sell the house, pay off the cabin and live on the island. Eventually, I'd arrived at the point where I wished to live on the sea; a way to live the simpler life I'd long sought. Often I'd tried to get her involved in sailing. She would try to act interested, but the fact of the matter was that it just wasn't for her. You either enjoy sailing or you don't. The harder I'd pushed for the simpler life, the more she'd clung to what she knew. She found refuge in our lifestyle; I found a prison. Perhaps part of the problem was that we had married at an age when neither of us had really formed solid ideas of our own values. Now that I was meeting couples who loved cruising together, I began thinking about the values that might make a future relationship work.

Friday, May 12 I arose to a thick fog. When the fog had nearly burned off I cast off the lines and motored down the inlet to fetch a buoy at Hamilton Island, also known as MacDonald Island. Over the past few days the dock had grown crowded, and I felt the growing need for solitude.

After *Pato* was safely moored to a buoy, I rowed ashore and dug a few clams at a nearby beach. Later, I went for a hike on a trail that led toward Camp Malibu. I followed the trail up the mountainside and into the forest, relishing the exercise. I came to a place where the trail crossed a thundering waterfall. A huge cedar log served as a bridge, affording a unique view as one crossed it. Looking upstream, the falls looked like many others; beautiful, but unremarkable. Looking downstream was incredible! I experienced a sense of vertigo, watching the powerful falls tumble toward the inlet below. Having crossed the creek, I followed a side trail that followed the creek up the mountainside. Eventually I found my way to an area that had been logged, and there I paused to enjoy the view. Far below I could see *Pato* nestled in her moorage next to the island. She looked safe and secure.

When I began to grow hungry, I made my way back down the trail and returned to *Pato*. That evening I dined on fresh clams, mussels, and oysters before turning in early. I would need to rise before sunrise to catch the first of the ebb at Malibu Rapids and bid the Princess farewell.

The Solo Sailor

The solo sailor, 'tis that which I be
  Sailing each day t'where my whim takes me

No one argues destination or course
  Nor to bitch when weather turns for the worse

Some who I meet on my vagabond way
  Envy what I've found, how I live each day

I hear them wish they were free as am I
  They feel but enslaved; they'll work 'till they die

Poignant the times on occasion I'd meet
  A loving couple, together at sea

They have what I have and oh so much more
  A friend and lover to keep the berth warm

Will I find love, the experiment grand?
  Dream or nightmare; take a chance, make a stand?

Will I find bliss? Will my future be good?
  Or lose what I never had, never could?

What really the risk, the worst come to be?
  The solo sailor will set out to sea.

Chapter Twelve

Saturday, May 13 It was my birthday. I'd completed another lap of the sun, and I was fifty-one years old.

I didn't want to be in my fifties. I much preferred to be in my forties. I thought about it, and resolved to just stay in my forties. First I was forty, then forty-one, two, three and so on through forty-eight, forty-nine … then forty-ten, and now I had reached forty-eleven. And what is age, really, but a number? It's often been said that you're as old as you feel. I maintain that you're as old as you act. I must be going on, oh, let's say about sixteen.

On a related note, I am often asked what I want to be when I grow up. It seems that most modern people confuse identity (to be) with profession (to do), and I think a lot of people measure their value as a human being in dollars and cents; I know that I had. For many years, I had felt like less of a person because I didn't have a prestigious, high paying job. I had spent most of my life wishing for a better career. Then, one day, I heard myself honestly answer the question, "What do you want to be when you grow up?" My answer: I want only to be happy.

On my forty-eleventh birthday, I awakened to the gift of a life-style that made me happy.

At 0515 hours I weighed anchor and made my way out to Malibu Rapids, which I reached at high slack water. I proceeded through the rapids and continued traveling down the reaches. I made good time, arriving in Egmont in time to hike to nearby Sechelt Rapids.

Sechelt Rapids produce a churning maelstrom generated by a sixteen knot ebb tide. It was mesmerizing to watch the ever-changing patterns in the current and eddies. Sechelt Rapids is a result of the combined waters of Sechelt, Salmon, and Narrows Inlets forcing their way through Skookumchuck Narrows at a point where the narrows are further restricted by the Sechelt Islets. The rapids have the appearance of a raging river, but are in fact salt water. The name Skookumchuck is derived from the words "skookum," meaning powerful, and "chuck," meaning water, in the local native tongue.

The ebb tide tends to be more powerful than the flood due to the combined flow from several creeks and rivers that empty into the inlets and bolster the flow. This coupled with a spring tide result in a spectacle of nature that leaves no doubt as to why the native people named it Skookumchuck.

Returning to *Pato*, I caught the last of the ebb out of the narrows and made sail. The northwesterly wind had risen to about seventeen knots and made for great sailing.

By this point in our journey, Slipper had become a vital part of the crew. She had discovered her favorite place to hunker down when the going got rough: right under the helm. When it was a little rough, she would lie forward of the binnacle. When it would grow rougher, she would move aft of it. This would place her as close to the center of *Pato*'s pitch and roll as you are likely to find. It seemed uncanny that she had found this very logical spot on her own. Although I respect her acumen, sometimes I find it a little annoying having her underfoot. But I take pity: when she lies there she sometimes looks … let's say less than happy.

Slipper would spend most days in the cockpit and most evenings lying on top of me. Anytime I sat or lay down, she would find her way onto my lap. This was generally pleasant, but sometimes could be a bit of a nuisance. When it was very hot, it could be uncomfortable, or if I was up and down a lot, I would always have to move her in order to get up. When under way or lying at anchor, she could have the run of the boat. When we were moored at a dock, she would be restricted below deck, as her curiosity can get the better of her and she is likely to wander the dock and other boats. She once managed to fall overboard at the marina. She is apparently a good swimmer, but I don't think she likes it. Often in our travels, people ask me how she liked sailing. Since she has never told me otherwise, I have to assume she loves it.

Once again, I did not have any particular destination in mind. As the hour grew late I found myself in the vicinity of Saltery Bay, which provides adequate shelter, so it was there that I dropped anchor at 1915 hours. When night fell, I stayed out on deck to watch the full moon rise. All in all it had been a good birthday.

Sunday, May 14, 1000 hours I got under way and made sail for nearby Westview. The northwesterly wind was blowing seventeen knots, perfect for sailing. I beat to windward, sailing a series of close reaches that *Pato* handled beautifully. The wind conveniently died just as I reached the point where I needed to douse the sails. As there is no anchorage at Westview, I made my way to the public marina and let a slip for the night. This was the first time I would stay at a marina on this voyage.

Due to the expense, I intended to spend few nights in marinas, instead lying at anchor whenever and wherever possible. I preferred remote coves devoid of other humans, for there I could find peace, tranquility, and privacy. I tend to shun the hustle and bustle of a dock. I tried to avoid anchoring close to power boats, as many would run their generators for long hours so they could watch their big-screen satellite TVs or blast their stereos while they slurped martinis and smoked Cuban cigars.

Why Westview? I was again in need of water and provisions and I needed to do laundry. The town provided all the necessary facilities. More importantly, when I'd last visited Westview I'd noticed that virtually every woman I saw was simply stunning. Daniel (who had jumped ship at Westview to return home by bus, ferry, and train) had made a similar observation. One can only handle so much natural beauty before thirsting for some beauty of another kind! The last time I'd visited Westview I was still married; this time I was newly divorced. Unfortunately, on this visit there was not one single beauty to be found, anywhere; none, nada, zip! Was I emitting some kind of pheromone that sent all of the local lovelies screaming off into the wilderness?

Oh well, at least I could complete my provisioning at the local Safeway. There I discovered another interesting custom. To get a shopping cart required that you leave a one dollar deposit, which was refunded when you returned the cart to the store. As I did not wish to leave a cart at the dock, nor walk the hill again, I carried some six bags of groceries to the dock. By the time I reached *Pato*, I would have gladly paid much more for the use of a cart. Near the dock I found several carts presumably left by other boaters who must have been much smarter or less scrupulous than I.

I topped off the water tank and did my laundry. With chores done, I treated myself to dinner at a local Thai restaurant. It was nice to eat something prepared by someone else, and Thai food has long been a favorite.

It had been a while since I'd had a strong phone signal, so I had been out of contact with home. I took advantage of the signal available in Westview to check in with friends and family. Jason and Nikki were doing well. I avoided asking them about Peewee, who, shortly before my departure, had packed up her clothes and cats and driven to her mom's home in Iowa, leaving her own house vacant. Peewee was trying to pick up the pieces of her life, and with her mom I knew she was in good hands. I hoped that she was finding strength there.

Next I contacted Daniel, who asked if I was having the time of my life, as he always does. I assured him that I was, but then it occurred to me that I was doing much more than merely having a great time ... I was taking the time to live. This was to become the theme of my journey, if not my life.

Monday, May 15 I cast off the lines at 0530 and motored up to Lund, where I stopped at a local bakery for a coffee injection and pastry. Lund is the terminus of the Trans-American Highway, which leads from Lund to the southern tip of South America. After having a nice walk, I again got under way. As there was no wind, I proceeded under power.

It was another beautiful spring day and the Sunshine Coast was really living up to its name. The southwest coast of mainland British Columbia lies in the rain shadow of mountainous Vancouver Island. As warm, moist marine air flows over the mountains, it rises and condenses to fall as rain on the island. By the time the air mass reaches the mainland, it has lost much of its moisture. Thus, the Sunshine Coast's moniker.

I continued up the coast and into Thulin Passage, which separates the Copeland Islands from the mainland. In the passage I decided to try my luck with a fishing lure. I was trolling along at two knots when I noticed a man sitting high on the rocks of an island, his dinghy on the shore below. As I watched, he walked to the edge of the precipice and commenced to play bagpipes! The mournful, haunting sound floating over the water and echoing off the shore sent chills up my spine, taking me to another place and time, a time long past that Peewee and I had shared.

We had been in Seattle to attend the annual Folk Life Festival at the Seattle Center. We had parked near the waterfront and were walking past an empty parking lot bordered by tall, concrete walls on three sides and open toward the water. In this amphitheatre were several people warming up with their bagpipes. They were not playing any tune in particular, yet the wall of sound they made had left a lasting memory.

I happened to glance at my GPS and saw that it read N50º00.00'. I was directly on the fiftieth parallel.

The unknown musician went on to play a number of tunes as I drifted on the current, having shut off *Pato*'s engine so as not to have its sound intrude on the serenity of the moment. I took this impromptu concert as a sign that I was just where I was supposed to be. When the bagpiper concluded his performance, I motored into the cove beneath his stage, where I dropped anchor, presumably for the night. I deployed the dinghy as the musician and his wife, whom I'd been unaware of, pulled away from shore. We met in our dinghies and I introduced myself to Jim and Linda. I expressed my heartfelt appreciation for his performance and invited them to visit aboard *Pato* for a while. Like me, they are unable to resist the temptation to look at other boats and accepted my invitation. After a brief but pleasant visit, they said farewell and left to return to their boat, hidden on the other side of the island.

I went for a short row between the islands and went ashore for a walk. The Copeland Islands are yet another marine park. Most yachters merely pass through the group on their way to Desolation Sound, as they offer few satisfactory anchorages. The park is used primarily by numerous kayakers, who appreciate the tranquility. I suspect that kayakers look upon all yachts in the same way we sailors (rag-baggers) look upon power boaters (stink-potters).

When I returned to *Pato*, I found that she was exposed to the wake, or wash as it is known in Canada, of every boat transiting the passage. Plenty of daylight remained, so I weighed anchor and set out for Desolation Sound.

Desolation Sound is located roughly half way up the inside of Vancouver Island and is a very popular destination for yachters and kayakers. The area boasts several large islands and numerous inlets, bays, and coves that offer anchorages. One can spend weeks in the area and lie in a different anchorage nearly every night. Due to its location mid-way up the inside, the water is usually relatively warm, allowing for a refreshing dip in the salt-chuck. The water rises and falls on the tide but doesn't flow through to any great extent, coming in from both north and south. Its situation allows the relatively stable mass of water to absorb warmth from the sun, which generally graces the area.

Two years prior, I'd visited Desolation Sound in *Laughing Wind*. I'd seen many of its wonders, but much remained to be seen. In reviewing my charts I saw that I had not yet visited Squirrel Cove on Cortes Island. The cove has an inner cove that provides a good anchorage, and what appeared to be a lake at its head. The chart had an area on the shore of the inner cove marked "IR," which means Indian reservation, or "First Nations Reserve" as they are called in Canada. I hoped to be exposed to native culture in my travels. The reserve, a secure anchorage, what I hoped was a swimming lake, and the fact that I'd never been there were reason enough to make Squirrel Cove my final destination for the day.

Motoring into Squirrel Cove, I passed a small village of the same name and noted that it appeared an interesting place to visit. It also had a government dock which would provide convenient access, so I decided to pay it a visit in the morning. The First Nations Reserve did not have a public dock, so I opted to not go ashore there. I continued on to the inner cove where I found several other yachts already at anchor. I found an open spot and dropped the anchor at 1715 hours. It had been a hot day and plenty of daylight remained, so I rowed over to the lake hoping for a swim. As I clambered over the rocks of the short creek leading to the lake, I noticed that the rocks were covered with barnacles and seaweed. I soon discovered that the "lake" was in fact a saltwater lagoon. So much for a refreshing dip in fresh water! I took a short dip in the salt-chuck and returned to *Pato* to have a bite of dinner and turn in for the night.

Tuesday, May 16 I got under way at 1000 hours and motored over to the village of Squirrel Cove, where I moored at to the government dock and went ashore. I walked to the nearby general store just to see if there were any supplies I couldn't live without.

Visiting a general store is like going back in time to the days before supermarkets, mega-malls, and home centers. It is refreshing to find groceries, hardware, marine supplies, fishing tackle, live bait, and post office under one roof. All that was missing was a brothel. I indulged in an ice-cream bar, one of the luxuries I often crave but am unable to keep aboard *Pato*.

At the store, I inquired about the nearby native village to find out if there was a museum or other cultural points of interest. I was told that the village was mostly residential and that the people valued their privacy. Most of the local arts and crafts shops were closed; perhaps it was still too early in the season. Having had a nice stroll, I went back to the dock and again got under way.

I motored *Pato* over to Refuge Cove on West Redonda Island. I'd stopped there for fuel two years prior in *Laughing Wind* and had thought that the rustic buildings surrounding the dock looked like something right out of a postcard. I recalled that they had a book exchange there and told myself that I was going there to replenish my supply of books, but in fact I was going there because I liked the feel of the place. The store that I'd thought so charming before seemed rather forlorn this time. It was under new ownership and they'd not yet stocked up for the season. I hope the new owners have found success. It is tragic when someone pursues their dream only to find that it eludes them.

After a brief visit, I again cast off and got under way. As I was making my way out of the cove, another boat, about a twenty-seven foot sailboat, was coming in. On deck were four men who looked like they were having way too much fun. Secured to the bow pulpit as a figurehead was an inflate-a-mate; an inflatable love doll with not one, not two but three of your favorite orifices! One could only imagine the debauchery that had transpired the night before. It brought to mind some of my own "missions" in earlier days, when I'd set out to save the world from all that is considered decent. It is gratifying to know that there are some who continue my crusade!

I turned my bow north and headed up Wis Channel, rounded Joyce Point, and entered Teakerne Arm. Teakerne Arm had been the terminus of my previous voyage to Desolation Sound and had left one of the fondest memories. At the head of the arm is a magnificent waterfall, which I feel rivals Chatterbox Falls in its splendor. The falls are flanked by vertical granite cliffs. At 1500 hours I anchored on a narrow shelf alongside one of the cliffs and stern-tied to a steel ring embedded in the rock. This left *Pato* lying parallel to the shore, only about fifty feet away. She was the only boat at the falls.

As I readied to go ashore, I realized that I'd forgotten my walking stick at Squirrel Cove. The stick was very precious to me. I'd found it, or it had found me, on Sucia Island in the San Juans two years before and I had spent countless hours burnishing it to a high sheen with a deer antler. I hoped that someone would find it and recognize that it was much more than an ordinary stick. I decided to return to Squirrel Cove the next day in the hope that someone had saved it for me.

I deployed the dinghy and rowed to the small dock near the falls, which is provided for dinghies and small boats. I followed the path which leads up from the dock to the top of the cliffs. In places, steps have been hewn from the solid rock. Often you will find yachts anchored directly under the falls, where the current from the stream prevents the boats from swinging on their rode. On a hot summer day it can be very refreshing to lay in the fall's constant mist, admire the rainbow which is ever present when the sun shines, and let the roar of the falls lull you to sleep. It is a sensory feast at Mother Nature's smorgasbord!

From atop the cliff, you can look down on any boats that may have anchored there and see the head of the tallest mast far below. I followed the path along the creek which feeds the falls. In one spot, a rope is provided to help you clamber across the face of a rock that provides no horizontal surface. The path leads to Cassel Lake, where one can leap from a granite monolith into deep green water. I stripped naked and took the plunge into cold, refreshing water. Once accustomed to the cold, I swam awhile and enjoyed feeling the use of muscles that had been long idle. Occasionally I'd climb up onto the rock again, to dive in or to bask in the sun on warm stone. I felt at one with nature, alone in this idyllic setting.

After my swim I made my way back down to the dock and returned to *Pato* for a bite. When I'd finished galley wench detail, I rowed over to a stone shelf west of the falls. On the granite shelf were a tiny lagoon and a few tidal pools where I could enjoy looking at sea-life up close. The granite was partially stained red from traces of iron in the stone, and partially green with algae. Lichens and moss nestled in crevasses. I examined the minutest of details in stones, sun-bleached wood, and other bits of flotsam scattered about. I tend to be oblivious to the small wonders of nature; large scale grandeur can monopolize my attention. Here I was reminded that pleasure can be found in the smallest or simplest of things.

Overlooking the water, and well above the high water mark, I found a fire pit. I've long loved the feeling of sitting by an open fire on a warm spring night. While I waited for the sun to set, I gathered driftwood for a fire.

As I waited, the tide began to rise. As it rose, it reached a point where the water of the sound had risen above the level of the little lagoon. Someone had strategically placed a few rocks in a crevasse through which the lagoon is filled, restricting the flow. When the tide reached a certain height, a reverse waterfall was created. The sound this small fall created is what many urban dwellers try to create in their backyard, in hopes of drowning the hustle and bustle that surrounds them. Here, the gentle whisper of the water took center stage. The only other sounds were the muted roar from the larger falls and the cries of gulls on the wing.

With nightfall, I lit my fire and grew mesmerized by the small blaze's flickering light, its sparks floating up toward stars twinkling in a clear sky. For the first time since I'd left home I felt a twinge of loneliness. The fire brought to mind times that Peewee and I had gone camping before we had kids. We'd had fun cooking meals in an old cast iron skillet over an open fire. Later, we'd loved camping with the kids in our Volkswagen Westphalia camper, "Gertrude I." There we were able to prepare meals on a stove but we always had a fire at night, and Nikki often would sit on my lap before the fire until she grew drowsy or fell asleep. Still later, our Herron Island cabin had a front yard firepit, where we'd enjoy a blaze while looking out over the water at lights on Johnson Point. Friends would often join us on Herron Island, and we'd drink ourselves stupid as we fed a fire from the never-ending supply of storm debris. More recently, just a few days before, I'd enjoyed a fire with other travelers at Princess Louisa. Outdoor fires had always been something to be shared with others, yet there I was by a fire, alone. I found myself longing for companionship, a feeling that surprised me. I usually tried to avoid human contact, seeking deserted anchorages specifically for their solitude.

The feeling soon passed as I doused the fire and returned to my refuge aboard *Pato Feo*.

Wednesday, May 17, 1030 hours I weighed anchor and made sail in the fresh northerly wind. I sailed a broad reach until I rounded Joyce Point where I fell off to a wing-n-wing run back to Squirrel Cove, hoping to retrieve my walking stick. After a brief but pleasant sail, I handed the sails and moored at the government dock. I inquired of my stick at the general store but, to my disappointment, no one there recalled having seen it. I had all but resigned myself to the loss of my trusty walking companion when I saw it propped up in a corner. Eagerly I gripped the smooth wooden shaft. Its slightly oval grip fit perfectly within my grasp, its slight angle aligning my wrist in an ergonomically correct position. The slender, frail-looking shaft possessed much greater strength than its appearance might suggest. I was glad to have my friend back.

Returning to the dock, I cast off and got under way once again. The wind had died down to nil, so I motored southeast past the Martin Islands, Mink Island, and into Tenedos Bay where I tossed out the hook at 1600 hours. I deployed the dinghy and rowed to a nearby stream at the head of the cove.

My chart showed a lake a short distance upstream. This time the stream proved to be freshwater, not salt as it had been in Squirrel Cove. With my trusty walking stick in hand, I followed the trail along the creek to the nearby lake. The lake was surrounded by wooded hills, the trees reflected on the mirror-like surface of its clear water. A logjam choked the head of the stream, and I clambered over the logs to strip and dive in. Leaping from the warm spring air into the cold water produced a delicious shock.

A peculiarity of male anatomy is that cold water can cause his member to shrink to ridiculously minute proportions; the colder the water, the greater the effect. This water was COLD! If the effect were any greater, I'd have known what it was like to be a woman! After a very short dip in the lake, I hiked a trail alongside the lake then returned to *Pato* for the evening.

Thursday, I opted to take a lay-day. It was a clear, hot day and I relished the idea of just hanging out and taking it easy. I spent the day skinny-dipping in the warm water of the bay and I went for a hike through the forest, where I was able to find shelter from the blazing sun. Later in the day, I took one last dip in the lake's cold water to rinse off the salt and sweat from my day off.

Friday, May 19 I prepared to get under way at 1000 hours. I had some trouble breaking the anchor free, but eventually brute force and ignorance prevailed and I made my way out of the bay. I motored over to nearby Predeaux Haven to have a look. Predeaux Haven is nestled in a group of islands and is one of Desolation Sound's more popular areas. It is quite scenic and offers many coves for anchorages. With the weekend nearly upon us, many boats had already arrived and many more were yet to come. It lacked the solitude I generally seek in my travels, but perhaps is a little quieter mid-week. Although there remained more of Desolation Sound to be seen, I was feeling the need to move on. Like many of nature's creatures, I was drawn north with the season.

Chapter Thirteen

And so it was that I left familiar waters and ventured into the unknown. OK, maybe not unknown to the world, but unknown to me.

I recalled the feeling of accomplishment that I'd experienced when I'd sailed Desolation Sound in *Laughing Wind*. For many Washington yachters, even cruising the San Juans is a lifelong dream. Many buy a yacht specifically for that purpose but never cast off their lines, meaning that Princess Louisa is but a fantasy and Desolation Sound as far away as paradise. When relating my story of that adventure I would put on an air of nonchalance, as if that journey was of little consequence to a sailor of my vast experience. Who was I kidding? That voyage had taxed the limit of my skills, but it had also taught me a great deal.

The day had grown hot and muggy, without a breath of wind as I left Predeaux Haven in my wake. Crossing Homfray Channel, I headed up Waddington Channel, which separates the mountainous islands of West Redonda and East Redonda. I continued up the channel until I reached Walsh Cove, where I set the hook and sterntied at 1400 hours.

I rowed around the cove for a while and went ashore. I found a nice bed of clams and filled a bucket with the critters looking forward to a dinner of fresh steamers.

I set out in search of the native pictographs I'd read about. Under a stone overhang, I found the first of several scattered around the cove. This one had faded to the point where it was unrecognizable. I went on to find several others, some entirely abstract (except perhaps to one who has studied the native culture and art). Others were quite clear as to their subject: deer, fish, a bow with arrow nocked in place, and what may have been a drying rack for fish and game.

The pictographs were generally found under an overhanging rock ledge, which would protect them from the weather, and well above the high tide mark. In places, the artist must have found himself practicing his art in a precarious position, perched high up on a cliff face. The pictographs appear to have been painted by fingertip, perhaps with a mixture of red ocher and some type of rendered animal fat.

I do not profess to know a great deal about the region's art and culture, but I find it fascinating to speculate about its significance and how it came to be. Why had the paintings been done? Were they of religious significance; part of a ceremony? Were they a way to tell others where game could be found? Were they simply an ancient version of a "no hunting or trespassing" sign? Some speculate that many of the pictographs in the area are hoaxes perpetrated for money when archeologists offered to pay natives to find them; if none could be found, they could be made. I choose to believe in their authenticity, preferring to see them as ancient art, not as modern graffiti.

Returning to *Pato*, I enjoyed a dinner of fresh steamed clams and turned in early. I needed to get an early start in order to take advantage of the tide as I continued my northerly trek.

Saturday, May 19 In the night, we had received a little rain. When I rose in the morning it was a cloudy day and a light drizzle was falling. It felt good to cool off after several days of hot weather.

I was under way by 0700 hours. I had laid a course that would take me through Yaculta and Dent Rapids and it was important that I reach them at or near slack water. Leaving Waddington Channel, I turned west, followed Pryce Channel, and passed north of Raza Island via Raza Passage. Reaching Calm Channel, I turned northwest and made my way into Yaculta Rapids, which lies between Sonora and Stuart Islands. I'd timed it perfectly and reached the rapids right at slack water. I threaded my way through the rapids and a small cluster of islands, then cleared Dent Rapids before the turn of the tide. I continued on my way along Cordero Channel to Hall Point, where I turned southwest down Nodales Channel.

Turning into Thurston Bay on Sonora Island, I began looking for a place to anchor for the night. I found a likely spot in a small cove east of Block Island. There was a nice looking beach at the head of the cove with a creek nearby.

As was my usual practice, I slowly entered the cove while reading the bottom on my depth sounder. It indicated twenty feet, fifteen feet, and then ten, at which point I began to turn and reverse my course. As I began my turn the sounder went to eight feet, and then it plunged to zero. *Pato* came to an abrupt stop. I quickly shifted to neutral, and then reverse. I throttled up and turned the helm from side to side, then tried rocking the boat in a vain attempt at freeing her. I checked for the point of the tide and was relieved to see that the tide would only fall about another foot before it would begin to rise. If you're gonna run hard aground, this is the way to do it; at or near low tide and on a sandy bottom.

While I waited for the tide to rise, I rowed out with my spare Danforth anchor, taking it to the limit of its rode and dropping it in about fifteen or twenty feet of water. Returning to *Pato*, I took a couple turns on the starboard genoa winch and tensioned the rode to prevent *Pato* from tipping as the tide continued to fall. Soon the boot stripe was about a foot free of the water and *Pato* was leaning slightly. Then the tide turned and began to rise. Eventually the water rose enough and *Pato* floated free. I retrieved my anchor and set out to find a more suitable spot to hunker down for the night.

On the other side of the bay I found a spot near a fishing trawler, where I dropped the hook at 1400 hours. Running aground had been a rather humbling experience, but no harm came of it, apart from a wound to my pride. But hey, if you haven't been aground, you haven't been around!

Sunday, May 21 I rose to an overcast sky. After the debacle of my grounding the day before, I got off to a slow start. I went ashore to walk the beaches and explore the forest. Again I looked in vain for mushrooms, but I did gather some seaweed from the rocks. I prepared a big pot of clam chowder with some of the clams I'd gathered in Walsh Cove. The seaweed would add a nice touch of color, flavor, and nutrition to the dish.

At 1350 hours I got under way. In reviewing my charts, I realized that I'd bypassed some rather interesting areas. I had not yet been travelling a full month and had made good time. I was in no particular hurry, as I planned to travel for several more months and had no firm plans about where I would go. Being beyond the midpoint of Vancouver Island, I'd reached the point where the flood tide flows from the north. This late in the day it was pointless to try to proceed against the flood, so I again turned south. There was a southeasterly breeze of only about five knots, but I shook 'em out (made sail) anyway. After the trials and tribulations of the day before, I found that sailing was good for my state of mind. After sailing for a short while, I motored east into Okisollo Channel. I made my way into Owen Bay where I anchored near the government dock at 1900 hours. I had a nice dinner of the chowder I'd prepared earlier in the day, read for a while, and called it a night.

Monday, May 22 My objective for the day was the nearby Octopus Islands. I had planned on getting an early start, but when I checked the chart I realized that I would be traversing Upper Rapids. The chart had the notation: "heavy overfall and eddies are extremely dangerous," so I prudently opted to wait for slack water, later in the day.

To kill time and get some exercise, I rowed over to the government dock to go ashore and take a walk. This dock had a rather ramshackle appearance about it, which was a bit of a surprise; most government docks I'd visited were well-maintained. This one had a number of derelict dinghies moored at it. They looked abandoned, despite a sign stating that there was a twenty-four hour limit. I found an open spot and made my dinghy fast to the pier.

Setting out from the head of the dock, I followed the dirt road leading south. I passed a few houses along the way, one of which had a small roadside hut with a sign boasting fresh baked bread. Another house looked like something out of a '60s cult film. I could picture flower children (hippies) laughing and dancing around the compound or tending their gardens, clouds of pot smoke wafting about their heads. Reaching the end of the road, I looked out over Okisollo Channel from the vantage point of a dock even more ramshackle than the government dock I'd just left behind.

Turning back, I retraced my steps, pausing to chat with a family at their rustic cabin. The cabin had been built of cedar salvaged from a huge log they'd found buried on their land. A hundred years ago loggers were interested primarily in Douglas fir, and cedar was often discarded as worthless. Over the years, wasted cedar logs became buried in the duff of the forest. Old growth cedar growing slowly in a thick forest is rich in oil that preserves it from decay. The second or third growth cedar that loggers harvest today doesn't possess this quality to the same degree because it has grown quickly in the abundant sunlight of the thinned woods. Hidden beneath the forest floor is a virtual gold mine of timber.

Returning to *Pato*, I weighed anchor at 1330 hours and set out for the Octopus Islands. I passed through Upper Rapids with no drama, as it was then slack water. I continued along Okisollo Channel for a few miles and past Hole in the Wall, before threading my way through the rock-strewn southern entrance to Waiatt Bay and the Octopus Islands. Once through the entrance, I turned north and headed for a cove I intended to be my anchorage.

To my dismay, when I reached the cove's mouth I saw a huge raft of sailboats and another of power yachts. I heard the flotillas' cacophony about the same time: stereos, jet skis, and Zodiacs comprehensively destroying any hope of tranquility. Clearly, this was not the place for me.

At the last minute I turned to port to skirt one of the islets that separated this cove from the next. The chart on my lap showed a submerged rock in the vicinity, so I paid close attention. To starboard, I spotted a light green patch of water, a sure-fire indication that a rock lies just beneath the water's surface. Satisfied that was the rock indicated on the chart, I was just beginning to shift my attention back to what lay ahead when CRASH! I ran up on the rock. Slipper dove down the companionway as if her tail was on fire. The whole boat shuddered, the rigging rang, and the bow dipped as she rebounded off of the rock. It seems that I had spotted A rock, not THE rock. I quickly engaged reverse and backed away from the offending rock.

Now that I'd been given conclusive evidence as to my location in relation to the rock, I proceeded into the next cove, giving the rock a much wider berth. I hoped that the blare of stereos had drowned out the resounding crash caused by *Pato*'s impact. I was more than a little embarrassed to have managed to run aground twice in three days and didn't relish the idea of having had an audience. If any of those in the cove had taken notice, at least I hope they had a good laugh. I was reminded of the words of one of the sailors I'd met at Princess Louisa: "There are two types of sailors, those who have run into a rock and those who will." I could now count myself among the former.

I made my way into the cove near the scene of my debacle and dropped the hook at 1530 hours. I reflected on the events of the last few days. When I'd run aground in Thurston Bay, I'd at least done it in the way I thought it was supposed to be done; a sandy bottom at or near low tide. I must have felt that I still needed to polish my skill, though, so I slammed into the rock for practice. I think I've got it now! Oh well, if you're gonna be stupid, you better be persistent!

I spent a few minutes pulling up the cabin sole to check the bilge and the keel mounting bolts. Thankfully, all was well. I was glad that *Pato*'s keel was cast iron, so any damage was purely cosmetic, apart from my twice wounded pride.

Keel Specifications

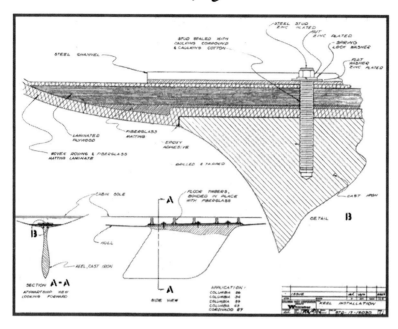

This is the design of *Pato Feo*'s fin keel, which allows for excellent maneuverability in tight confines. The keel is cast iron and weighs 4,700 pounds. I can personally vouch for the integrity of the design, having run aground twice and hit a rock once in the course of my voyage!

Tuesday, May 23 And so it was that I found myself in the Octopus Islands. I'd left my home port of Port Orchard only thirty days before and had travelled 606 nautical miles. In one month I'd had many adventures, and I eagerly anticipated what lay ahead.

I spent the morning wandering the cove's shore before weighing anchor at 1230 hours, in order to reach Surge Narrows at slack water. An interesting thing about Okisollo Chanel is that, once inside, every exit is hindered by narrows or rapids and their powerful currents.

A light rain was falling as I motored out of Waiatt Bay and headed down Okisollo Channel. I made good time and reached Surge Narrows a little early, so I needed to kill time. I hovered behind Antonio Point until the current had subsided sufficiently for me to continue, and then I cleared the narrows and Beazley Pass before making my way down Hoskyn Channel.

By the time I reached Sutil Channel, which lies at the northern end of the Strait of Georgia, the southwesterly wind had risen to twenty-five knots plus. Short, steep seas had developed in the long fetch extending the length of the strait and *Pato* began pounding so hard that I found it difficult to maintain a speed of more than one knot.

My destination for the day was Gorge Harbor on Cortes Island. I'd planned on going south until I cleared Marina Island and its outlying reef before turning into the gorge, but soon I realized that it was going to be a long struggle to make any southing against these winds and seas. So much for Plan "A." Plan "B" was to quarter the seas and make for Uganda Passage to the north of Marina Island. Plan "C," if you could call it that, was to fall off to port until the seas were off my starboard quarter, and see what shelter might fall under my bow.

With the wind and seas on my quarter, I was finally able to make some way. Ahead lay Quartz Bay on the western shore of Cortes Island. As the skies began to clear, an incredible rainbow led me to my refuge for the night. It was nearly flat and broad with the most vibrant colors imaginable, and it lay directly in my path. With a sense of relief I made my way into Quartz Bay. At 1900 hours I anchored in front of a picturesque little cabin fronted by a lawn of thick moss.

The day had been a long grind, the culmination of a few hard days that had somewhat shaken my confidence. Funny how running aground a few times can have that effect. To add insult to injury my GPS, a veteran of many a voyage, died. With it went hundreds of waypoints I'd entered in preparation for this trip. I was glad that I hadn't opted to get a GPS chart plotter, as I would have been much more dependent on it. It also served as a graphic reminder of why it is vital to carry paper charts. Still I had grown to rely heavily on my handheld GPS and felt it was a vital piece of equipment. A replacement would need to be found, although I didn't relish the idea of having to spend the money.

Wednesday, May 24 I listened to the morning weather report on the VHF. Environment Canada forecast southeasterly winds of ten to fifteen knots; perfect sailing conditions. At 1000 hours, I set out once again for Gorge Harbor. I didn't have many miles to make and eagerly looked forward to a nice day after the trials of the previous few.

A light shower was falling as I made sail at the mouth of the harbor and I began beating to weather. In a repeat of the previous day's weather, the wind rose to twenty-five knots and the seas began to build.

Expecting fifteen knots, I'd raised a full press of canvas. *Pato* was overpowered but due to the sea-state, I was reluctant to go forward and reef the main. I opted to tough it out until I reached the safety of the weather shore of Marina Island, where I handed the sails. Conditions were difficult and I did not want to put myself on a lee shore, so I decided to motor through Uganda Pass to reach Gorge Harbor.

I noticed that my propeller didn't seem to be getting a very good bite and began to suspect that it was fouled with flotsam or kelp. I reversed hard to try dislodging whatever may have caught below, and it seemed to help. Could that explain why I'd had so much difficulty making headway the day before?

I began to question whether it was advisable for me to venture out on the big pond (i.e. the Pacific). Was *Pato* up to the task? Was I? After all, her sails were growing a little long in the tooth. The batten pockets on the main and mizzen were becoming a little ragged and the leech on the mains'l was a little chafed by the topping lift. Also, I was still getting some flutter on the foot of the jib. And what of the seas? If I was having difficulties here on the inside, what would I have on the outside? Here I was fighting wind-waves. There I might encounter wind-waves as bad as these on top of ocean swells, or perhaps cross-seas (where the wind-waves come from a different direction than the swells). I may have felt more confident if I had a crew. Fortunately, there was still quite a bit of time before I would need to make my final decision.

Once I'd cleared Uganda Pass, I turned into the narrow gorge that serves as the entrance to Gorge Harbor and lends the harbor its name. To port, I saw the pictographs that grace its steep stone walls. I made my way into the harbor and at 1600 hours I anchored in a small cluster of other boats near the fuel dock.

Thursday, May 25 In the morning I took care of some engine maintenance before taking *Pato* over to the dock for fuel and water. Tanks full, I steered *Pato* to nearby Manson's Landing, where I moored her at the government dock and set out for the village on foot. It felt good to stretch my legs, get a small dose of civilization, and partake of a local eatery's fare. I wandered around the village a bit and shopped some of the local establishments, more to get a feel for the place than to actually buy anything. Hippies live, eh?

With a full belly, I returned to *Pato* and cast off. My next port of call would be Campbell River, where I hoped to find a replacement for my GPS. It was fortunate that if it had to fail, at least it was in the vicinity of such a town.

When I cleared the harbor, the southeasterly wind was a pleasant ten knots, so I made sail. I plotted a course which would carry me well clear of Whilby Shoals off Cape Mudge before turning north into Discovery Passage. The wind built to a comfortable twenty knots and, sailing a beam reach, *Pato* was behaving beautifully. After all the trials and tribulations of the past few days, it felt wonderful to be back in sync with my boat. Even Slipper seemed more relaxed than she had been in a few days.

I reached Discovery Passage at slack water and fell off into a run up the passage. I sailed past Campbell River and had a look at its waterfront. Although I needed to shop there I didn't intend to stay in a marina, opting instead to anchor across the passage in Gowland Harbor on Quadra Island. I had considered Quathiaski Cove, which would have been convenient for access to the ferry that would carry me to Campbell River, but it just looked too busy for my taste. When I'd cleared Gowland and Steep Islands, I rounded up and doused the sails before motoring into Gowland Harbor. I found a nice spot to anchor near Stag Island, where I dropped the hook at 2000 hours.

In the morning, I rowed over to a nearby dock at a youth camp and went ashore. I walked through the camp and found my way to the main road. I started walking south toward Quathiaski Cove, but I hadn't gone far when an old-timer in a beatup pick-'em-up truck offered me a ride. I gratefully accepted and enjoyed a nice talk with him. I asked what I should expect to pay for ferry fare. His reply was to hand me a pass. He dropped me off at the ferry landing and continued on his way. As he drove off, I realized that I'd not even gotten his name. Kindness of the type he'd shown had become rare in the world. He had just helped rekindle my faith in humanity.

After a short ferry ride across the passage to Campbell River, I walked downtown in search of a marine supply store. I soon found a chandlery, and they said they would be happy order me a new GPS at an exorbitant price. I thanked them and said I'd consider it. Crossing the street to a fishing tackle shop, I asked them if they knew where else I might find one. To my surprise, they said that they had the model I wanted in stock, and at a great price. With my new GPS in hand, I wandered around town. I happened across an old-fashioned barber shop and, because I was getting a little shaggy, stopped in for a cut. It was fun to hang out with the locals and swap lies. Finally, I stopped off for some provisions before returning to the ferry.

When I arrived back in Quathiaski Cove, I wandered through a few art galleries and gift shops. In one shop, I met a local woman named Terry. We struck up a conversation. Terry told me a little about life on Quadra Island, and I told her a little about my travels.

She told me that I'd arrived the weekend of Quadra Island's May Day celebration, and she encouraged me to stay a few days so I could attend. It was not difficult for her to convince me.

Terry offered me a ride back to the dock and asked if I'd care to join her for dinner. Since I needed to row my provisions out to *Pato* before going anywhere, I invited her to come along and meet Slipper. She gladly accepted.

After a brief tour of *Pato*, Terry and I returned to shore and drove to her place, where she prepared a simple meal. Her home was one of a group of humble little cabins in the woods. I gratefully accepted her offer of the use of her bathtub while she cooked. While travelling, it is not practical to bathe every day. Often I have to settle for a spit-bath. I am convinced that after a few days without a shower, our bodies develop a natural odor that is not offensive, but then I've been wrong before. Perhaps she was trying to tell me something.

After dinner we went for a walk and she introduced me to a pair of draft-horses that lived in the pasture behind her home. When we'd finished our walk, Terry lit incense (which she uses for aroma-therapy) and entertained me with a musical performance played on hammered brass bowls. The bowls are played in somewhat the same manner as when one makes a tone with a moist finger on the rim of a wine glass. It was a haunting and fascinating performance.

Saturday, I stood down for the day. I'd been on the go so much that it felt good to simply lie low. I read a lot, played with Slipper, and cleaned up the cabin a bit.

Sunday morning, as arranged, Terry picked me up and we drove over to Rebecca Spit on the other side of the island. We wandered among the May Day Festival crowd, many of whom had donned colorful costumes. A troupe of bagpipers marching in full regalia started off the festivities, which culminated with children performing a traditional dance around a maypole. It was the sort of joyous celebration that makes small town living so much more gratifying than life in suburbia or a big city.

I will always be grateful to Terry and the anonymous stranger in the truck for making me feel so welcome in their community. Terry and I agreed to stay in touch from time to time; she was interested in hearing about my ongoing journey. My visit to Quadra Island had been most memorable.

Monday May 29 It was time to move on, and I was under way at 0630 hours in order to ride the last of the ebb through Seymour Narrows. I didn't plan on covering many miles and had considered going only as far as Small Inlet in Kanish Bay on northern Quadra Island. Daniel had once anchored there and said it was quite beautiful. When I got there, the tide was too low to enter the inlet, so I opted for Granite Bay. I anchored there at 1000 hours and rowed over to a derelict dock, where I moored my dinghy and set out for a hike.

My chart showed a couple of lakes that held promise of a refreshing dip; I never miss an opportunity to go swimming. I followed the road until I found the trailhead leading east. I passed a couple beaver ponds where I had to step over trees that had been felled by the critters. Eventually, I found my way to the lake where I was able to fulfill my wish for a swim.

On my return trip, I took time to search for mushrooms and was rewarded with a nice harvest of oyster mushrooms, which seemed to be about the only kind to be found that spring. I also indulged my interest in edible native plants by comparing specimens I found along the way with pictures in the pocket guide I carried.

Near the end of the trail, I was drawn into the woods by the sound of a waterfall. The scene was postcard perfect; stream plunging over and through moss-covered granite boulders, sunlight beaming through trees, and mist creating a brilliant rainbow. The unique feature of this scene was that the stream, which had a fairly substantial flow of water, travelled only about twenty feet from the falls before simply vanishing into the ground! The water percolated down through decomposed granite soil to reemerge on the other side of the trail some distance away.

By the time I got back to the dock I'd hiked quite a few miles and my legs felt great; tired, but great. In the morning I would embark on the next leg of my journey. Quadra Island had been yet another of many highlights I'd seen along the way, and I knew that many more lay ahead.

Chapter Fifteen

Tuesday, May 30 I arose to another beautiful spring day; blue sky and a fair wind. I'd reached another turning point in my travels. When I'd left Port Orchard, I'd headed nearly due north to Canada. Since arriving in Canadian waters I'd been travelling in a generally northwesterly direction. I'd now reached a point where my travels would carry me west, toward the setting sun.

At 0936 hours, I weighed anchor and made my way out of Granite Bay and then Kanish Bay. My destination for the day was Forward Harbor, and I would be sailing the imposing Johnstone Strait. I consulted my *Tides and Currents Table*. It indicated that the peak flow of the ebb tide, 1.3 knots, occurred at 0855 hours. The tide would turn at 1356 hours, reaching a peak of 0.3 knots at 1521 hours. These predictions for Johnstone Strait Central were based on the current station located at Port Neville. I wondered why everyone made such a big fuss about Johnstone Strait and didn't bother to open up my volume entitled *Sailing Directions*, which has an entire chapter dedicated to the strait. After all, I would be riding the ebb for four hours, and when the tide turned I would only be bucking a current of 0.3 knots. Even ol' *Pato* could easily overcome such a current.

At the mouth of the harbor I made sail in a lovely southeasterly breeze of fifteen knots and sailed wing-n-wing until I reached Chatham Point. Rounding the point, the wind rose to twenty-five knots and I sailed a broad reach while enjoying the spectacular scenery along the strait. Fair winds, smooth seas, and a clear sky: What more could a sailor desire? *Pato* and I were enjoying one of those magical days under sail.

With the boost of the ebb flow, we were making very good time and soon I found myself at the end of West Thurlow Island, where I was to make my turn toward Forward Harbor. I was making such good time and enjoying sailing so much that I decided to continue on to Port Neville instead. I cleared Helmicken Island via Race Passage, and off Salmon Bay I checked to see how my progress was toward my new objective. I had only seven nautical miles to go. According to my knot-meter I was making six knots through the water and my compass indicated a heading of 274° magnetic. I compared these numbers with my GPS. It indicated a track of 094° magnetic and a speed of two knots. I was going backwards!

I checked and rechecked my *Tides and Currents Table* to see if I'd read the wrong page and found that I'd read it correctly. How could it be that I was only seven miles from the current station and encountering currents that differed so drastically from those at the station? Is it possible that the current station on which all of the secondary station's calculations are based could have been placed where there is no appreciable current? Could it be that the Canadian Hydrographic Service had made a blunder, or was I just stupid? I concluded it was likely that I am just stupid. After all, I had in my possession a copy of *Sailing Directions*, which comprehensively documents in great detail the peculiarities and subtleties of the currents in the strait, yet I had chosen not to consult that vital publication.

Realizing that every minute I was being swept further from my destination, I decided to revert to my original destination of Forward Harbor. I would have to backtrack some distance to Chancellor Channel, which would lead me to Forward Harbor via Wellbore Channel and Whirlpool Rapids. I rounded up and began beating to weather, now aided by the current. I reached the rapids at slack water, proceeded through, and made my way into Forward Harbor where I set the hook at 1900 hours.

I'd had a wonderful day of sailing and had learned a new lesson. It is foolish to embark on a voyage of this nature without having proper charts and publications. It is equally foolish to possess said publications and not use them.

Wednesday, May 31, 1000 hours I motored out Sunderland Channel to Johnstone Strait, where I made sail in the fifteen knot southeasterly wind. The weather was mostly sunny and warm and made for pleasant sailing. The wind soon rose to twenty knots and, sailing a broad reach, I flew up the strait to the Broken Islands, where I turned north-east up into Havannah Channel. I was now beating to weather in twenty-five knots and *Pato* was performing great. I proceeded under sail through a couple of tight spots in the channel where there were a number of well-marked rocks. I considered choosing Burial Cove as my anchorage for the night but instead opted for Matilpi Settlement, on the other side of the channel. I'd read somewhere that there were ruins of the native settlement to be explored at Matilpi. I nosed into the gap between the Indian Islands but decided it was a little tight for an anchorage. Instead, I chose a notch to the south of the two islands. I set the hook at 1600 hours and settled in for the night.

In the morning I rowed ashore in search of the ruins of the settlement. All I was able to find was one collapsed shack, lots of beach glass, and what looked like a shell midden. A midden is a refuse heap where generations of First Nation's peoples discarded their trash, consisting mostly of shells and bones. Many amateur archeologists have scoured these middens for artifacts such as stone tools, jewelry, and art. This practice has now been banned and is restricted to archeologists who have obtained a proper permit.

Thursday, June 1 the weather took a turn for the worse; blustery winds, low clouds, and rain. In this rough weather I was a little uneasy about my anchorage, but I had missed the tide and could not reach Chatham Channel by slack water. I weighed anchor and motored to the head of Boughey Bay while trolling for any wayward fish that might be in the area. As usual, I posed no threat to the fish population. Most fish are smarter than me and cleverly avoid my lure. Reaching the end of the bay I reversed course and motored to Burial Cove, where I anchored for the night.

Friday, June 2 I timed my departure to reach Chatham Channel at high slack water, 0900 hours. I motored the few miles to the channel and proceeded through, using the range markers to stay within the channel's navigable area.

Continuing on my way, I soon reached Minstrel Island. I moored at the government dock and went ashore for a look around. There was a large resort consisting of many buildings, all abandoned. There had once been a hotel, a restaurant, and many other attractions, but all were now left to the elements and scavengers. It was disheartening to wander through this virtual ghost town, where someone must have once pursued their dream; a dream now lost.

Leaving Minstrel Island behind, I motored through The Blow Hole, which separates Minstrel Island from East Cracroft Island. I made my way to Lagoon Cove where there is another resort, this one much more humble but thriving.

I'd heard that the resort's proprietor had a nightly happy hour at which he served fresh-caught prawns. Although I'd only left Quadra Island a few days before, I was feeling the need for some camaraderie, and the temptation of fresh seafood was enough to bring me to the dock. I'd considered anchoring out, but I didn't feel it would be right to partake of the resort's happy hour hospitality and not pay for use of their dock. Besides, I'm a big eater and figured that I could easily consume enough prawns to justify the cost.

At the appointed hour, I joined the other patrons at the head of the dock. The happy hour was a BYOB affair and I brought a few "barley-pops" (non-alcoholic beers), while the others brought their favorite libations. Bill, the proprietor, told a number of amusing stories, and then we all mingled and swapped lies. When happy hour was over, we continued conversations as we made our way back to our boats.

I met Kelly and Linda on *Blues Power*, their beautiful ketch, as well as their travelling companions on *Riki-Tiki-Tavi*, a newly completed trimaran. *Riki-Tiki-Tavi*'s owners were a couple who had toiled for many years to complete the project. She was beautifully appointed to the minutest detail and finished in the most hideous shade of green imaginable!

Yet another couple was marooned at the dock, awaiting a new raw water pump for their engine. The stranded woman's frustration became apparent the next morning. I was awakened by the sweet chirping of sparrows as they darted about the marina. I was having a cup of coffee in the cockpit, enjoying their songs, when the unfortunate woman walked by. I bid her good morning and remarked about the sweet birds. She stated a willingness to bite off their heads, throw their corpses to the dock, and stomp them into a bloody stain!

There, at a dock in the remote backwaters of British Columbia, were several couples cruising together. One couple lived aboard, one had built their dream together, and yet another was marooned. All seemed to be getting on well, although I could only imagine what a strain the marooned couple must be under. I wondered if the day would ever come when I would be able to share cruising with the woman I loved; a woman I hadn't yet met, and thought that perhaps I never would.

Saturday, June 3 I tossed off the lines at 1100 hours, made my way out of Lagoon Cove, and made sail. I motor-sailed through the cut between Minstrel and Turnour Islands, then continued to Knight Inlet. I killed the engine, fell off into a broad reach, and flew west down the inlet riding the ebb and a twenty knot southeasterly wind. For a while I was making twelve knots! It was a pleasure to watch the beautiful scenery pass by as Slipper and I enjoyed another wonderful day under sail.

Ahead lay the Broughton Group, an archipelago consisting of dozens of islands, islets, rocks, passages, coves, and bays. In short the Broughtons offer plenty of opportunities to hone your navigational skills. To get an idea of how this area looks on a chart, put a cracker on the floor and stomp on it! It is as if the entire coast of British Columbia has crumbled. I'd be hard pressed to define where the mainland ends and the islands begin.

I took advantage of my brief time in Knight Inlet's lower reaches to brace myself for the challenges that lay ahead. Reaching the end of the inlet, I opted to pass south of a small group of islands, the largest of which was Midsummer Island. There I turned north and sailed a close reach up Retreat Passage, which carried me into the heart of the Broughton's.

At this point in my journey, I'd been through many of the destinations many cruisers dream of – the San Juans, the Gulf Islands, Princess Louisa Inlet, Desolation Sound – and now I'd reached The Broughton Group.

I made my way into Grebe Cove on Bonwick Island, where I anchored in a notch behind a small islet at 1730 hours. I had the entire cove to myself, which assured my privacy.

Sunday, June 4 In the morning, I rowed out and set my crab pot before crossing the cove to an abandoned log landing. From there I set out to hike the logging roads that would lead me into the heart of the island. It had been awhile since I'd had the opportunity to really get some exercise, so I set out with a vengeance.

The day grew sunny and hot as I made my way across the island, and soon I was covered in sweat. Along the way, I saw signs of bears having sharpened their claws on trees and found some bear scat that contained the claws of an unfortunate beaver. I grew a little uneasy about the presence of bears and, knowing bears to be shy of human contact, began to sing aloud as I continued my hike. Anyone who has ever heard me sing will attest to the fact that my voice could send the fiercest of creatures scurrying for cover!

My hike concluded without incident, and I turned my attention to eating. I'd foraged trailside for mushrooms and had found a few, but none I could conclusively identify as edible. Returning to the dinghy, I headed for *Pato*, pausing to check my crab pot on the way. I was rewarded with a couple of Dungeness for dinner. I decided to spend another night in Grebe Cove.

Later that evening, when darkness had fallen, I amused myself by stirring up phosphorescence in the water. I rowed around the remote cove, causing the water to twinkle with each dip of the oars and my wake to glow eerily in the darkness. Even answering the call of nature was an experience. Peeing over the rail, the pee hitting the water had an effect like fireworks bursting in the water. When flushing the head later that night, the inlet hose glowed greenish white and glitter-like sparkles swirled down the bowl. It was like a flashback to the seventies!

Monday, June 5, 1030 hours I got under way, setting out to explore the Broughtons. I would stop off at Echo Bay for some milk and eggs; a guy can't live on fresh crab alone! I made my way under power up Retreat Passage, then threaded carefully through the Fox Group and rock-strewn Cramer Passage, to Echo Bay.

I entered the bay and saw, to port, a small resort consisting of little more than a dock, a gift shop, and a few houseboats. The entire resort was built on floats moored at the base of a granite wall decorated with several pictographs. To starboard was a more sophisticated looking facility with a fuel dock and store. I moored at the smaller resort's dock at 1430 hours and visited the gift shop, where I bought a birthday present for Nicole, who would soon be turning twenty.

I had a nice visit with the lady running the gift shop, Carol, who told me about some local attractions and the history of the area. Carol took great delight in pointing out the pictographs on the stone wall behind her shop. She also gave me some insight regarding bears.

It seems that in Canada more people are mauled by black bears than by the more-feared grizzlies. This happens partly because many people do not show due respect to the smaller black bears. People often take their dogs along on hikes, thinking their dogs will protect them from bears. What really happens is that a dog barks and agitates a bear until it charges, at which point the dog runs and hides behind its master!

On Carol's recommendation, I anchored out in the bay and rowed over to the government dock to walk to Billy Proctor's museum. Billy and his museum are well known all over this part of the coast. Billy had found his first native artifact at the age of seven and, some seventy years later, was still collecting. His museum has a huge assortment of stone tools made of obsidian, chert, and basalt and still more tools of bone, antler, and wood. There are numerous pieces of jewelry and art and hundreds, if not thousands, of trading beads. There is fragments of beach glass of every conceivable color, displayed alongside dozens of liquor and opium bottles, the latter left by Chinese immigrants who had been smuggled through the area.

There were artifacts of logging and fishing activities, as well as many other items of Canadian lore too numerous to mention. Outside is a small pond with a beautiful boardwalk and railing made entirely of driftwood. Billy's museum is nearly always open; if the door is locked, just knock on the door of his house and he will open the museum for you, and share stories of the past. He has a coffee can in which you can place donations to help defray the cost of maintaining his museum. I regretted that I only had five dollars to contribute, as the value received seemed worth so much more.

I passed through the schoolyard, where children were running a relay race, then set out on a trail that led off into the woods. Alongside the trail runs a black poly pipe, laid to carry water to the resort. The pipe had been repaired in a number of places where bears had bitten through it. Apparently this is a common problem, but no one seems to know why bears feel an urge to bite the pipes; perhaps they are just being mischievous.

Eventually I found my way to the water source. It consisted of no more than a pile of rocks, creating a crude dam across a small creek. This formed a tiny pond, which was covered with a net to keep out leaves and debris. From this pond, gravity carried water through the bear-perforated pipe to the resort. Water from the tap was the color of piss, and Carol recommended that I filter the water as I filled my tank, to prevent forest debris and bugs from contaminating my tank. I will say that the water had a wonderful flavor, even if it was a bit chewy!

That evening, at her invitation, I joined the other cruisers at the houseboat of Carol and her husband, Jerry, for a happy hour. I presented them with a picture I'd drawn of their boat, in ink on a shelf fungus. They were delighted with this humble gift.

Tuesday, June 6, 2006 Yea, that's right; the date was 666, my second favorite number! I weighed anchor and made my way over to the larger resort to get milk and eggs and to mail Nicole's birthday present. The main part of the resort was built on a huge concrete pontoon that had once been part of the Hood Canal floating bridge, an engineering feat situated in my home waters of Washington State. Some years back, the bridge had been heavily damaged in a heavy storm and some portions had sunk. It was a bit of a surprise to find a piece of my local history here in the remote waters of British Columbia.

After a pleasant visit to Echo Bay, I set out to explore the Broughtons. At 1230 hours, I left the bay and made sail under clear skies and a nice northwesterly breeze of ten knots. I sailed a beam reach as far as Horsford Point, where I rounded up into a close reach and headed west along Fife Sound. The wind built to twenty knots as I continued along the sound, and sailing was great.

As I sailed the sound, I watched a helicopter fight a fire on one of the islands, dropping water from the huge bucket suspended below it by a cable. Fortunately, it appeared to be a small blaze that was soon extinguished.

I passed north of a small cluster of islands, where I turned to port and into a series of tight passages that separated the islands. I'd selected a potential anchorage on my chart, but when I sailed into the cove I found it was already occupied by a couple of power yachts. I continued on my way, hoping to find a cove I could have to myself. I motored through a narrow cut between Eden and Insect Islands before again setting sail, west through Misty Passage. I beat to weather, having to tack several times in this narrow passage. I really enjoy the challenge of exploring these small, tight passages, particularly under sail. Soon I reached Joe Cove, where I found a nice anchorage and dropped the hook at 1830 hours. Only one other boat, a sailboat, shared the cove. Across the cove was a beach which appeared to be a midden, so I decided that in the morning I would row over and have a look.

Wednesday, June 7 In the morning, I rowed around the cove exploring the shoreline and eventually making my way to the beach I'd spotted the night before. As I'd suspected, it was a shell midden, confirmed by a sign posted on the shore.

I followed a trail into the forest for a while in order to stretch my legs. I found several rotten logs that had apparently been torn apart by bears in search of grubs, so again I burst out in song to keep the pesky critters at bay. Returning to the beach, I looked carefully along the water's edge in hopes of finding some artifacts such as trading beads. Although I didn't find any beads, I did find a chip of obsidian that had likely been leftover from making a tool or weapon. I also found a piece of bone, which appeared to have been fashioned into an awl.

I spent the rest of the day much as I'd spent the morning, just hanging out, relaxing, and amusing myself. I decided to spend another night in Joe Cove. That night when darkness fell, I sat on deck in the warm spring air and looked to the heavens. It's like an entirely different universe when you see it away from the glow of city lights. Several meteors streaked across the night sky. The moon shone large and bright, its reflection on the water providing stark contrast to the trees' black silhouettes. The stars and planets seemed to have been multiplied and magnified a thousand fold. Our own Milky Way galaxy became a broad brushstroke across the sky. Neither paint nor film could ever capture these images in a way that would do them justice. Later that night, in my warm, cozy cabin I thought again that life is good, if you take the time to live it!

Thursday, June 8 I set out to continue my meandering course through the Broughtons. The morning sky was overcast, and gale force winds were forecast for the afternoon. The course I'd plotted would carry me into Queen Charlotte Strait, so I got underway a little early to be sure I'd arrive in more sheltered waters before it came to blow.

At 0930 I made sail just outside Joe Cove and motor-sailed out to the strait in order to briefly charge my house batteries. When I reached the strait, I shut off the engine and sailed a close reach into the fifteen knot northwesterly breeze. The wind gradually built to twenty-five knots, and *Pato* took it in stride. Clearing the Polkinghorne Islands, I fell off and sailed a broad reach up Wells Passage. I sailed into Tracey Harbor and had a look around before continuing on my way. Reaching Patrick Passage, I turned east and followed the shoreline of Atkinson Island on a downwind run to Sullivan Bay.

I sailed across the bay to have a look at the village of Sullivan Bay before sailing into a notch behind Atkinson Island, where I sailed onto the hook. I let the wind carry me back to set the anchor before I handed the sails at 1830 hours. Sailing onto and off of the anchor is something I like to do from time to time, partly for the challenge but also to train myself for the day when my auxiliary engine may fail and leave me with no choice but to do so. It had been yet another great day of sailing.

Friday, June 9 I weighed anchor and motored across the bay to visit the village of Sullivan Bay, built entirely on floats. There are a number of vacation homes, a restaurant, a store, and a fuel dock. There is a signpost with arrows pointing toward various ports around the world and stating their distance from Sullivan Bay. I enjoyed a brief stroll along the docks, wondering what it would be like living in a town afloat. I bought a few provisions before casting off at 1100 hours. The wind had eased to five knots overnight, and I took advantage of the light breeze by leaving the dock under sail.

Leaving Sullivan Bay, I sailed west along Patrick Passage before turning northeast up Grappler Sound. The northwesterly wind rose to a comfortable ten knots, and I sailed a close reach as I rode the flood up the sound. It was nice to sail along at a slow pace and watch the beautiful scenery glide by.

At Watson Point I turned east through a narrow cut to reach Kenneth Passage. Ahead lay a range of mountains which, to me, suggested the form of a reclining woman. Two peaks formed her breasts, the foothills her legs and the line of her neck leading to her turned-away face. A creek cascaded from a gorge which represented the gap between her legs. As I continued along the passage, the image sharpened before my eyes. I imagined an Indian maiden presenting herself to me in a fertility rite. As a sometimes artist, I often see things others may not: many may see nothing more than beautiful mountains, but then who hasn't seen images in the clouds? Many might suggest that I'd been too long without a woman, but that notion would cheapen the beauty I perceived. There is nothing on this earth more beautiful than the female form.

Leaving Kenneth Passage, I entered MacKenzie Sound and sailed a broad reach eastward along the length of the sound to its end. At 1800 hours I dropped the anchor near a grassy meadow on the sound's north shore.

A short row away a large creek emptied into the sound. I'd heard some ancient petroglyphs could be found along the creek, and I set out in search of them. The chart showed that the creek originated at MacKenzie Lake a short distance up-stream, and I looked forward to a dip in its waters. I followed the southern shore of the creek, but the trail soon disappeared. I was forced to turn back. Perhaps I'd have better luck along the northern shore, but it was getting a little late so I put off further exploration until the next day.

As I rowed back to *Pato*, I was drawn to a grassy meadow on the shore. I decided to stop there and see what there was to see. As I neared shore, I glanced over my shoulder to gauge my approach. There, not more than fifty feet away, was a mother bear and her cub! I quickly reversed course and put some distance between myself and the bears. Mother bears are notoriously protective of their young, and I didn't want her to view me as a threat. She cast a wary eye in my direction, as if to make it clear I was not welcome. I stood off shore at a comfortable distance, and they went back about the business of foraging for a meal. Thankfully, I wasn't on the menu!

Saturday, June 10, 0930 hours I got under way for points unknown. Under partly sunny skies, I motored out of MacKenzie Sound against the flood. At Kenneth Passage, I looked back to say farewell to the mountain maiden. On the shore I saw another bear, turning over rocks and feasting on the tiny crabs scurrying from their disturbed refuge.

I took a quick turn through Turnbull Cove before continuing on to Grappler Sound. Off the entrance to Hopetown Passage I decided to troll and was rewarded with a small rockfish. Continuing on my way, I passed through Dunsany Passage to reach Sutlej Channel. A pleasant northwesterly breeze of five knots was blowing, so I made sail on a broad reach and travelled east along the channel. As I sailed, I considered my options for an anchorage and decided on Cypress Harbor. The wind conveniently died when I was about a mile or so from the harbor, and I doused the sails.

As I handed the sails, I noticed that I'd lost two battens on the mains'l and that the foot flutter on the jib had taken a toll. Although I'd found a solution to the problem some time before, it seems I'd waited too long. The sail had torn along the line of stitches at the foot. I applied a "band-aid" in the form of some sail tape and fitted my spare battens to the main.

When I'd finished my repairs and fitted the sail covers, I noticed that the engine temperature was alarmingly high and the alternator light on. I immediately shut down the engine. Before I even went below to look in the engine compartment, I knew that I'd broken the alternator belt, which also turns the raw water pump. I'd replaced the belt not long before my departure from Port Orchard, and fortunately I'd saved the old belt as a spare. In a short time I'd fitted the replacement.

I'd just restarted *Pato's* engine when I saw another vessel, a high-speed power boat, change course and make their way straight for me. By observing our vessels' motion relative to the mountains, I was able to determine that we were on a collision course. The power boat was off my starboard bow, meaning they were the "stand-on," or "privileged" vessel, and I was the "give-way," or "burdened" vessel. I changed course and then reduced speed, yet we remained on a collision course. I was just preparing to unleash a barrage of blue words (of which few would argue I have a very comprehensive vocabulary) when the boat turned on a flashing blue light and pulled alongside. It turned out that we hadn't been on a collision course but an intercept course, which is exactly the same but completely different.

The boat was a high-speed patrol boat of the Royal Canadian Mounted Police, and they wished to check my customs papers.

I was disappointed to see that the RCMP were not wearing bright-red woolen coats and midnight-blue riding breeches (let alone the cool hats), made famous to American children by the cartoon character Dudley Do-right. Remember him? He was big in the 1960s.

Despite their relatively drab uniforms, these real-life RCMP officers were very polite, and in fact quite pleasant. While one of them checked my papers, another frisked my first mate and scratched behind her ears. If my mate hadn't been of the feline persuasion, it might have been a violation of her civil rights and she would have been screaming instead of purring.

The RCMP officers were interested in hearing about my travels, and I was perhaps a little jealous that they were able to make a living zooming around in a boat in one of the world's most beautiful areas.

They were quick to remind me that the area wasn't always as pleasant as it is on a warm spring day, and that many people they visited were not so pleased to see them. After a brief but cordial visit, they spotted a vessel engaged in fishing and zoomed off to call on its captain.

Free to be on my way, I motored into Cypress Harbor and tossed out the hook. It had been a rather eventful day. That night as I lay in my bunk, I contemplated where I would wander next, but I decided to put off the decision until morning. One mustn't be hasty about these things.

Chapter Seventeen

Monday, June 11 A foggy morning … For the casual mariner, fog provides reason enough to stay in your warm bunk and enjoy another pot of coffee. With no rigid agenda, I had the luxury of being able to relax and wait for the fog to clear.

As I nursed my coffee, I contemplated where I might wander next. From where I lay at anchor, in Cypress Harbor on Broughton Island, there were a number of possibilities. I was still considering running down the outside of Vancouver Island, and if I chose to do that I was already as far north as I would travel. But the fifty-first parallel was enticingly close, just up Wakeman Sound, and I thought how nice it would be when relating my story to say I'd been as far north as the fifty-first parallel; it's a nice round number. It then occurred to me that when this big blue ball we call home came to be, it didn't have black lines drawn around it with numbers like 51º 00.00 affixed. It was only my ego asking me to go north.

Still, Wakeman Sound would likely be a beautiful place. But then the same could be said for virtually every waterway I had seen, would see, or could see on this voyage. Is it possible that I was becoming jaded? Had I seen so much scenic beauty that it was becoming mundane?

And then there were the practical considerations. Wakeman Sound is a dead end with no anchorages to be found along its twelve-mile length. If I were to venture up the sound, I would need to double back and find an anchorage before darkness fell. This was entirely feasible, and so Wakeman Sound remained a possibility. I pondered my other options.

Tribune Channel would carry me around Gilford Island. A couple of sounds branch off the channel, and they could provide more interesting cruising and, possibly, anchorages. That route would lead me farther into the wilds of Canada, and it was not a dead end. Hmm, this looked like a good possibility.

Then it occurred to me that I didn't have to choose one path over the other. I could do both if I wished; or neither for that matter.

By 1030 hours, the fog had burned off sufficiently. I'd still not made up my mind as to where I was going, so I put the decision before the navigation committee, consisting of me, Slipper and *Pato*. I abstained from the vote and Slipper was non-committal, so the decision was *Pato*'s alone.

Pato's decision was to venture into Tribune Channel. The northwesterly wind was only about five knots, so I proceeded under power. I briefly lost track of where I was and found that I'd strayed into Simoom Sound. I was going to correct course, but the sound looked so inviting that I decided to stay the course; sometimes you have to play the hand you're dealt. I reduced speed and trolled for a while as I made my way deeper into the sound. As usual, no fish accepted my invitation to dinner. At the end of the sound lies McIntosh Bay, where I tossed out the hook between a small cluster of islands at 1630 hours. I set my crab pot in the bay, hoping I would have better luck crabbing than I had fishing.

Once settled, I decided to check the engine compartment. Much to my chagrin, the spare alternator belt I'd just fitted was showing signs of accelerated wear. I realized that I would have to find a replacement as soon as possible. This meant that I would have to abandon my plans of following Tribune Channel. Instead, I'd seek the nearest outpost of civilization.

Monday, June 12 I weighed anchor, pausing to retrieve my crab pot as I left McIntosh Bay. I retraced my path out of Simoom Sound and laid a course back to Echo Bay, where I knew I could either find a belt or find out where to get one.

The air was calm so I had to motor, with my fingers crossed that the belt wouldn't fail completely. Fortunately, I made it, and as I made my way into the bay, I was pleased to see the unmistakable form of *Riki-Tiki-Tavi* moored at the dock. Lying at anchor in the bay was *Blues Power*. It was nice to see the friends I'd met at Lagoon Cove.

I stopped at the dock to ask where I might find a belt. Jerry suggested Port McNeill on Vancouver Island. I was uneasy about venturing across Queen Charlotte Strait with a somewhat ragged belt, but what choice did I have? Clark from *Riki-Tiki-Tavi* overheard our conversation and mentioned that he had a spare belt that might fit. He retrieved the belt and I compared it to the old one. It was a little wider, but it looked like it would work.

I motored across the bay to anchor, and then set about the business of fitting the new belt. I found that it would work fine, provided I removed one of the three mounting bolts that held the raw water pump. That very bolt was causing me all of this grief: It was in such close proximity that if the belt were not extremely tight, it would come in contact and damage the belt.

Kelly and Linda invited me to join them aboard *Blues Power* for a lasagna dinner, and of course I eagerly accepted. They must have thought that an unattached man was incapable of properly feeding himself, or perhaps they just enjoyed my company. As I was rowing over, it began to rain. As our dinner baked, we were treated to a nice thunderstorm.

When you are lying safely in a secure harbor, it can be a real treat to see nature's fury; much different from its impact when you are out fighting the elements. The thunderstorm passed and was followed by a beautiful rainbow, which we enjoyed as we ate the delicious dinner Linda had prepared. As I prepared to row back to *Pato*, we were treated to a spectacular sunset.

As I lay in my bunk that night, I reflected on how sweet this life was compared to what I'd left behind. The wonders of nature, the camaraderie with fellow cruisers, and the freedom to live each day as I chose made me feel that all was well in my world.

Tuesday, June 13, 1030 hours I set out for Port McNeill, motoring out Cramer and Arrow Passages in a light, patchy fog. When I reached Norwell Channel the fog appeared to be lifting, so I ventured out into Queen Charlotte Strait.

No sooner had I entered the strait than the fog came down with a vengeance, reducing visibility to about an eighth of a mile. I briefly pondered turning back, but the passages I'd just left behind were narrow and strewn with rocks. The path ahead was open water with few obstacles. I'd already entered waypoints and a route in my GPS, and following those would carry me all the way to my destination of Port McNeill. I chose to carry on, sounding my horn as I continued on my way. I had no desire to be run down by a passing freighter or cruise ship.

The fog lifted before I reached my next waypoint, just off Donegal Head on Malcolm Island. Under bright, sunny skies I made my way up Cormorant Channel, which separates Malcolm Island from Cormorant Island.

Entering Port McNeill at 1630 hours, I ventured into the municipal marina and looked for an open slip. The marina was a zoo! Many boats were jockeying for position, and there were few open spots. I was directed by radio to a tight spot between two other boats on the main pier. Normally, one would enter the slip with it on your starboard side, but I find it difficult to dock *Pato* starboard-to due to the prop-walk of her right-hand screw, so I chose to maneuver in a way that would let me dock port-to.

I motored slowly into the fairway separating the piers and performed a short-turn. A short-turn can be accomplished with some boats in an area not much larger than the boats length; *Pato* is such a boat. I executed this maneuver by putting the helm hard-a-starboard while still making way. I then engaged reverse while putting the helm hard-a-port. This brought the boat to a stop while allowing the prop-walk to spin the boat. I then shifted to forward, put the helm hard-a-starboard, and with a brief burst of power used the prop-wash against the rudder to finish the turn. I then nosed into the slip at an acute angle, and engaged reverse to bring the boat to a stop and walk the stern to port, which allowed me to slot *Pato* into the slip with inches to spare.

While I was performing these maneuvers, a crowd of nervous boaters had gathered in the fear that I would crash into one or more of their boats, but as I made *Pato* fast to the pier, I got a resounding round of applause. I adopted an air of nonchalance; shucks folks, 'twern't nuthin'!

I was immediately reminded why I tend to shun marinas; it was a madhouse! There were too many people and too much activity for my taste. At the end of the dock was a power yacht that looked like a cruise ship. Two guys were actually jogging laps on deck! Why? Because they could! I suppose they wouldn't want to get their exercise ashore, where they might be exposed to anything or anyone resembling normal.

Seeing the very wealthy in their element reminded me that there is a distinct difference between being wealthy and being rich. The richest people I've ever known had financial resources that bordered on poverty, but still led rich, fulfilling lives. I'd be lying if I said I didn't wish for more money. Who doesn't? But if this was what having a lot of money could do for you, count me out!

Port McNeill was the closest thing to a town I'd visited since Campbell River, so I took advantage of its services and facilities. My first order of business was to find a replacement alternator belt. The belt that Clark had given me was doing just fine with the offending bolt removed, but I was reluctant to continue my journey without a spare or two. I soon found an auto parts store that had the belts in stock; mission accomplished. Next I set out to do my laundry. While my laundry dried, I had a bite to eat at a café across the street from the marina. I completed my tasks as efficiently as possible so I could get under way again the next day. One night in this marina would be plenty, thank you! Don't get me wrong: The marina had nice facilities, the people were friendly, and the town was fine, but the whole thing was just too much of a shock for me after so much solitude.

Wednesday, June 14 I restocked my provisions and bought some "barley pop" as a treat. (Some might say that having beer without alcohol is like having sex without a partner, but I like them better than soda-pop.) At 1400 hours I cast off and left Port McNeill behind.

My objective for the day was the nearby Pierce Islands, which comprise another marine park. The wind was nearly calm, so sailing was not an option. With few miles to travel, I motored along slowly while again trying my luck (what luck?) fishing. Along the way, I passed close in along the shore of Alert Bay on Cormorant Island. I'd heard that it was a pleasant village to visit, but chose to save it for another day. Continuing on my way, I soon arrived at my destination, the Pierce Islands. I entered a protected area in the middle of the various islands of the archipelago. At 1830 hours I anchored in a spot where I had a view of a beautiful mountain range to the north. To the east, through a gap in the islands, I could see the Plumper Islands; through another gap to the west, Cormorant Channel.

The scenic beauty inspired me to pick up my pencil and pad and sketch my impressions of the vista before me. It had been many years since I'd painted watercolor landscapes and seascapes, and I was still trying to find an outlet for my artistic urges. Living and travelling on a boat there is no shortage of inspiration, but many of my creations were just not practical or possible in the tight confines afforded by *Pato*. I hoped to be able to draw something which, in the future, could carry me back to this place and time.

It is often said that one picture is worth a thousand words. A few remarkable artists are able to capture emotion in a picture or sculpture; unfortunately, I'm not one of them. After drawing for a while, I came to realize that while a picture could capture a visual image, the written word could capture feelings and emotions much more effectively. I began to write a poem, my first in close to forty years. In poetry, I found an outlet for my feelings of joy and sorrow, hope and fear. My first effort at poetry, "Taking the Time to Live," from which this book gets its name, was the result. It is unlikely to receive critical acclaim, but then I wrote it for an audience of one; myself.

Chapter Eighteen

Friday, June 16 was a day like many others I'd experienced in the nearly two months I'd been away from home. I'd spent a couple days in the Pierce Islands, although I hadn't gone ashore. I'd stayed aboard *Pato*, immersing myself in art and poetry. After a leisurely morning I set out for nearby Alert Bay. I'd heard that a native village and museum there were worth a visit. Little did I know what an impact Alert Bay would have on me and my journey.

I pulled into the municipal marina adjacent to the ferry dock and made *Pato* fast in a vacant slip. I stopped off at the marina office to see if I could stay for a few hours while visiting the village. I was told that for short stays, I should use the government dock on the other side of the ferry landing; however, it turned out that the marina's moorage fee was very reasonable. I decided to let a slip for the night, which would allow me to thoroughly charge *Pato*'s batteries and visit the village without any time constraints.

At the head of the dock, I was faced with the choice of turning left toward the native village or right toward the Canadian village. Turning to port, I strolled along the waterfront toward the 'Namgis Nation's reserve. I paused briefly at a gift shop that specialized in art and jewelry inspired by native art. There I inquired about the museum. The U'mista, as it is called, could be seen at the far end of the bay near the old marina, now operated by the tribe.

Continuing on my way I soon came to a small hut where a native carver, Jason, was practicing his trade using traditional tools. He was just starting an orca carving in his tribe's unique style on his preferred medium, yellow cedar. He showed me some of his completed work as well as some made by his cousin, Steven. Steven's work is widely recognized, and he had received commissions from as far away as Japan. My son, Jason, had a birthday approaching and I decided that the carving this Jason was working on would be the perfect gift. He assured me it would be done in a day or two.

As I visited with Jason, a number of his friends and relatives dropped by. Kevin, one of Jason's cousins, invited me to attend a naming ceremony and feast that evening at the "Big House," where a baby would be given his native name. The Big House is a community center based on their tribe's traditional communal dwellings. I eagerly accepted the invitation. It would be an honor to observe a native ceremony that was not staged for tourists.

With plans for the evening made, I reversed course and headed for the village of Alert Bay. Since I would have to hang around for a few days, waiting for my carving to be completed, I opted to see the U'mista some other time. I also needed to look for a bank so I could withdraw the money for the carving.

Just past the ferry landing, I strolled into the village. It consisted of a few gift shops and art galleries as well as a combined grocery, hardware, tackle, and marine supply.

I was just about to enter the store to ask where I might find a bank when an attractive woman approached. She had dark, flowing hair, high cheekbones, and deep brown eyes. She had the purposeful stride of someone who knew her way around town; perhaps she was a member of the 'Namgis tribe. Our eyes met and we held each other's gaze for a moment. We smiled. As she approached I held the door for her, and as we entered I inquired about the bank.

Her name was Judy, and as it turned out, she worked at the bank and was on her lunch break. She kindly offered to show me the way. As she bought her lunch and we strolled the short distance to the bank, we got acquainted. I asked if she was going to attend the ceremony that evening, but she had other plans. I asked if she might care to get a bite sometime that weekend. She said she would love to, but she would be very busy all weekend at a regional soccer tournament that pits various First Nations tribes' teams against one another.

I know little of the ways of women, and I thought this was her way of blowing me off. Instead, she invited me to hang out with her at the tournament! Wow, I had a date!

After I concluded my business at the bank, I killed some time wandering around town before making my way to the Big House for the ceremony. Adjacent to the Big House is a totem pole which at 173 feet is purported to be the tallest in the world, although I understand that other communities also claim this distinction.

I met Kevin at the door and we filed in with the others to find a seat on the bleachers that flanked the walls. The structure was built of huge cedar poles. Those above the entrance and the podium were intricately carved and painted. In the center of the amphitheater was an open firepit.

The ceremony began when a man stepped forward and one by one called the tribal elders forward in their native tongue. When the elders were assembled, several men began beating on a log, which served as a ceremonial drum. The audience joined the elders in song as dancers in full tribal regalia entered the arena one by one.

Kevin described the intricacies of some of the dance moves that represented different animal spirits. Many of the audience danced at the perimeter of the arena. Among them was a boy of only three or four years old, who danced with skill and enthusiasm that belied his years.

Eventually, the child for whom the ceremony was being held was brought before the elders by his father to receive his name, which unfortunately escapes me. (If I could recall it, I doubt I could pronounce it.)

At the conclusion of the ceremony, several tables were brought in and a feast laid out. When Kevin had invited me to the ceremony, I had feared that if I participated in the feast there might not be enough food to go around; after-all, I have a huge appetite. As the food was laid out on the tables, my fears evaporated.

All manner of seafood, many familiar and many new to my palate, had been prepared in the traditional ways of their people. Along with mountains of salmon, crab, halibut, clams, and mussels were herring eggs still attached to the eel grass on which they had been laid, as well as other items which I couldn't even begin to identify. Venison and elk meat were also on the menu, as were other native delicacies gleaned from the forest, sea, and shore.

All dishes were drizzled with prodigious amounts of ooligan grease, which is considered a staple among the native peoples of the Pacific coastal area. This grease is the oil rendered from the eulachon, a small fish somewhat like a herring, which is so oily that it has been referred to as the candlefish. It is said that one can put a wick in a eulachon and use it as a candle. There was once a trail across Vancouver Island called the Grease Trail, which generations had used in the trade of this commodity. Wars had even been fought over this grease. The natives use it with everything, from fish and game to fruit and nuts. Today, some people keep jars of grease in their refrigerators, to spread on their morning toast, as we might use butter. I didn't find its flavor particularly appealing. Perhaps it's an acquired taste.

After I'd eaten my fill, I continued to eat until I reached my threshold of pain. Then I ate more. Still the food kept coming! My fear that there would not be enough for all clearly had been unfounded. It was with drooping eyes that I waddled back to *Pato* to sleep off the food orgy. It had been an incredible honor to have observed this ceremony, which gave me a memory I will cherish forever.

Saturday morning, as arranged, I met Judy at the soccer field. She was setting up a booth to sell her herbal teas, which she blended from a number of native plants. She had studied the medicinal benefits of these various plants, and her recipes addressed health issues ranging from heart conditions to menstrual cramps. The teas are also delicious. I helped her set up her booth and we chatted while she plied her trade.

Throughout the day we got to know each other. Judy was part French-Canadian and part Cree Indian. She had recently broken up with her boyfriend, and since I was recently divorced we had some common ground. It had been over a year since Peewee and I had separated. I felt I was ready to move on.

Several of Judy's friends and acquaintances stopped by to visit and all made me feel welcome. Among the friends who stopped by was Steven, who offered to drive me around to see a little more of the island. It didn't take long, as Cormorant Island is not large. We returned to the tournament just as an ambulance was pulling away. We learned that one of the local players had suddenly collapsed and died on the field. He was forty years of age. A somber mood replaced the jovial atmosphere that had prevailed earlier in the day.

Sunday, the games resumed and the home team was victorious over all comers. When the trophy was awarded to the team captain, he sobbed as he dedicated their triumph to their fallen brother.

I'd had a wonderful weekend in Alert Bay and had spent not less than three days at the marina! This would remain the longest marina stay of my entire voyage. Judy and I had hit it off, and I'd invited her to go sailing. She'd never been sailing and was eager to give it a try, but she wouldn't be free until Thursday. I was in no hurry to move on, so Thursday it would be.

On Monday, I picked up the now-completed carving from Jason and dropped it in the mail to my son. It was a beautiful piece of art, and I knew he would be delighted.

Next I visited the U'mista, the tribal museum that had first caught my attention when I'd arrived in Alert Bay. In the Kwak'wala tongue (once spoken by the 'Kwakwawaka'wakw, or Kwak'wala-speaking people, including the Namgis), the word "u'mista" meant something akin to "return."

In the days of Canadian expansion and settlement of the west, the government had made every effort to assimilate the natives into Canadian society, the method being to comprehensively destroy every remnant of the native culture. Tribal languages, religions, and governments were oppressed or banned outright. Potlatch, a vital tribal tradition throughout western North America, was forbidden. A potlatch was a gathering of tribes for trade, negotiation, competition, and ceremonial gift-giving. Canada's government hadn't wanted tribes to interact with one another and possibly organize a resistance. Many tribes' art and artifacts were destroyed, or confiscated and added to the collections of the tribes' oppressors. The U'mista had been built in 1980 to study, preserve, and display artifacts that had been returned to their rightful owners from museums and private collections around the world.

Outside the building were a number of newly carved totem poles, as well as several in various stages of decay that were stored under a canopy awaiting restoration. Traditionally, totem poles were not restored, but allowed to decay and return to the earth. However, it has become vital to preserve the few remaining examples. It is a paradox that the tradition of decay must be broken to preserve the tradition of creation.

The U'mista's double entrance doors were huge carved cedar panels painted in traditional, bright colors. In a large, climate controlled room was an incredible collection of intricate ceremonial masks, some of which would transform from the form of one creature to another by moving articulated parts. These were the most striking examples of the artistry and craftsmanship practiced by these people. Carving remains a vital part of their culture.

There were also remnants of "coppers," which had been their way of showing wealth and status. Coppers were about the size and shape of a medieval knight's shield. It is believed that copper was introduced to the tribe by early Spanish explorers; perhaps the first coppers were fashioned from the remains of a shipwreck. Later the tribe traded for the commodity or smelted their own. Scraps of the metal would be hammered and riveted together to produce the end product. The coppers would then be brought to a potlatch, where they would be ceremonially gifted to another tribe, either in whole or in part. The more a tribe gave, the greater their wealth and status.

There were also examples of dugout canoes crafted from huge cedar logs, some of which could carry as many as thirty or forty people. Outside were a few canoes in various stages of completion.

A few short steps from the entrance to the U'mista stands a huge reminder of the oppression of the natives, in the form of a large brick building. The dilapidated structure had been the Catholic school where generations of native young, stripped from their families, were brutalized and forced to conform to the ways of the white man. It would seem to be a monument to sorrow.

It is gratifying to see the revival of traditions among the 'Namgis people, as well as many other tribes across the land. The U'mista plays a vital part in this revival.

Monday, June 19 Having a few days before I could go sailing with Judy, I took a day sail to Sointula on Malcolm Island. Along the way, my mizzen sail developed a small tear. My suit of sails was really beginning to show its age.

When I returned to Alert Bay that night, I anchored near the western shore. That evening at sunset, a young man beat his drum and in his native tongue sang songs of mourning for the man who had died at the soccer tournament. His song, carried across the water, brought tears to my eyes.

I spent the next couple of days just hanging around town and seeing what there was to see. I hiked to the "Gator Gardens," a beautiful marsh in the middle of the island. A boardwalk traverses the marsh, allowing easy access.

Ever since I'd arrived in Alert Bay, I'd felt like I was home. I began to inquire about availability of land to buy. I had a desire to find a piece of dirt to call my own. My search led me back to Steven, who had shown me around the island on Saturday. As it turned out, he was considering subdividing his property. He expressed a willingness to sell the lower part.

The land was heavily wooded with large spruce, fir, and cedar trees. It was steeply sloped to the south, with a beautiful view of the water and Vancouver Island. I could see myself building a tiny cabin in which I could spend my time ashore. We agreed on a price and shook hands, which to me is as binding as a signature on a contract. I'd found my home! (Or so I thought.) Over the next couple days, I looked at the Island not as a visitor, but as a resident. When I'd set out on my journey, I'd not known where my travels would take me. I'd not in my wildest dreams hoped to find a home.

Thursday finally arrived, and I picked Judy up at the government dock at 0900 hours. We motored through the Pierce and Plumper Islands, and then continued on to Telegraph Cove on Vancouver Island. We visited the whale museum, which had a number of skeletons of the various species that frequent these waters. As we were leaving the museum, a sound at the mouth of the cove drew our attention. There, within sight of the museum dedicated to them we could see a humpback whale, the first I'd seen on my journey.

Leaving Telegraph Cove behind, we laid a course back to Alert Bay. The wind started to build and we made sail. The fifteen knot northwesterly breeze was perfect for Judy's first sailing experience. and she loved it. I showed her some of the finer points of sailing in an attempt to dazzle her with my wealth of knowledge and skill. It had already been a perfect day, and I thought to myself that it couldn't get any better, unless we got to see some dolphins or porpoises. As if on cue, they appeared! As we were beating to weather and making five or six knots, a group of Pacific blue-sided dolphins frolicked in our bow wave for a while. While *Pato* sailed herself, I joined Judy on the foredeck to enjoy their performance up close. We sailed back into Alert Bay and dropped the hook under sail. I retrieved the crab pot that I'd set that morning and we dined on fresh Dungeness that evening. Later, I rowed Judy ashore and walked her home. As we strolled we made plans to go sailing again on Sunday. It had been a magical day and had whetted our appetite for more.

I spent the next couple of days helping Steven clear the property lines of "my" land in preparation for the survey that was needed to facilitate the subdivision. In my mind, I began to build my tiny house nestled into the hillside. Not being familiar with the legalities of buying land in Canada, I was a little uneasy about the transfer of funds and title, but in a leap of faith I continued moving forward. I loved the feel of the land and its setting. With each passing day I felt more a part of the community.

Sunday, June 25 Judy joined me to go for another sail. Unfortunately, we had no wind. We motored to Hanson Island, where we dropped the hook in a sheltered cove. We deployed the dinghy and rowed ashore to explore the shoreline and woods. Judy insisted on trying her hand at the oars and proved very capable of rowing in circles. Returning to *Pato*, I prepared us a nice meal and we chatted in the cockpit until well after dark.

Judy had never slept aboard and was eager to give it a try. I know what you're thinking, but it wasn't that way at all! The forward cabin provides more than adequate accommodations for guests. Had she tried to take advantage of me, I was prepared to put up a valiant (but not too valiant) fight to preserve my virtue. As it was, she was able to resist temptation (damn!) and I did my best impersonation of a gentleman. In the morning, we returned to Alert Bay.

Along the way, I told Judy of my intended land purchase. She expressed her dismay that Steven hadn't offered it to her first; after all, she had been the one who had found the land for Steven in the first place. She and Steven had been close friends since her arrival in Alert Bay and, being the newcomer, I did not wish to come between friends. I told Judy that if she had the means and desire to buy the land, I would step aside and allow her to do so.

Thus began a protracted three-way dance between Steven, Judy, and me. She secured financing and agreed to meet Steven's price. My heart sank as I realized that my dream of owning this piece of the earth would not come to fruition. I resigned myself to the fact that it was not meant to be and started making plans to continue my journey. I planned to reprovision, and depart in a few days.

A couple of days later, I was reading in the cockpit when I heard someone shout my name from the shore. It was Steven. He asked whether I still wanted to buy his land! I expressed my eagerness to proceed with the purchase although I was a little perplexed. What had happened with Judy? As it turned out, I wasn't the only one who had had romantic thoughts about Judy. Although Steven didn't come right out and say it, it became apparent that he was interested in her too. To further complicate matters, it seems she hadn't completely broken up with her boyfriend. The plot thickened! Steven had come to realize that it might not be a good idea to sell Judy the land. He would rather sell it to me.

I was beginning to have my reservations about the purchase, but I opted to proceed with caution. The survey was not yet completed and there were documents to be signed at City Hall pertaining to the subdivision, so everything went into a holding pattern.

Monday, July 10 I motored over to Port McNeill for fuel and to go to a larger bank where I could transfer money from home. I quickly accomplished my mission and set out once again for Alert Bay. On the return trip I ran into Dean and Dianne on *Talisman*. I'd not seen them since Princess Louisa and we swapped a few lies about our travels. As usual, Dean was dragging a fishing lure and, as usual, having the success that eluded me.

Later that evening I met Rob and Dorothy. We struck up a fast friendship and found that we shared many common interests, including unusual art, the environment, and native culture.

Dorothy's two step-daughters from her first marriage were coming for a visit, and she and Rob asked if they could charter *Pato* for a day. At that time I didn't have a license, so I couldn't legally do charters, but I offered to take the family out for the day in exchange for their company. I never miss an opportunity to meet available women, and Rob told me the girls were quite attractive.

Tuesday evening I stopped by to meet Johna and Truela and to firm up our plans. Rob made the introductions and I said to them, "I'm pleased to meet you guys." Truela informed me in no uncertain terms that they were not guys; they were women. Strike one. With our plans made for the next day, I prepared to take my leave so they could catch up on things. At the door I said I looked forward to spending the next day with "you girls." Truela reminded me that they were women. Strike two. Clearly she had issues. Did I mention she was a redhead? Her fiery disposition matched her hair.

Wednesday, July 12 I picked up my guests at the government dock at 1300 hours, and we made sail. The wind was southeasterly at about fifteen knots with gusts of up to twenty-five knots. We fell off and headed northwest around Cormorant Island, under broken clouds with occasional squalls. Sailing was great and the family made good company.

To say that Truela was a militant feminist would be a gross understatement; one might even say she was a femi-nazi. Once I concluded that anything I said would be considered a sexist statement, I decided I might as well fuel the fire. I pulled out the stops and fired a barrage of my very best. We had great fun with it. Johna, also a redhead, had never been sailing before and she thoroughly enjoyed it. She was somewhat soft spoken, and for the most part was happy to sit back and watch Truela and I exchange barbs.

Dorothy had prepared us a nice lunch, which we shared as we made our way around the island. At one point, a fishing boat turned across our bow to pass starboard to starboard. He broke several rules of the road and I was forced to take evasive action to avoid a collision. As we passed I shouted, "I have redheads aboard and I ain't afraid to use 'em!" Of course they could not hear my shout and were probably unaware of our existence.

I dropped my guests off at the government dock at 1700 hours and made my way back to my preferred anchorage to drop the hook for the night. It had been a most entertaining day, and I was relieved to have survived my sparring with Truela with my testicles intact!

Throughout my stay at Alert Bay, I'd spent most days at anchor, rowing ashore and mooring my dinghy at the old marina which is operated by the 'Namgis tribe. I would generally moor my dinghy at the base of the ramp. When I returned for it one day, I found it in a different location than I'd left it. I thought perhaps I'd left it in an inconvenient spot, and thought no more of it. The next time I returned, it was where I'd left it, but was made fast to the pier in a different manner. A few days later, it was not at the dock at all! I spotted it on the beach, awash and full of trash. Now I was less than happy. I asked some people on the beach if they'd seen who had left my dinghy there and was told that three teenage girls had been fooling around in it. The next time I used the dock, I left a note on the thwart that they were welcome to use my dinghy, but to please show a little respect by returning it to where they got it. Their response was to shred my note and leave more trash in my dinghy; so much for trying to reason with teenagers.

My dinghy was of little monetary value, in fact it was worth less than nothing, but it was essential for me to be able to come and go ashore. To protect this vital piece of hardware, I moved *Pato* to an anchorage closer to the municipal dock, where I hoped my dinghy would be more secure. When I returned, my dinghy was nowhere to be seen! Now I was getting pissed! I set out on foot to the old dock where I found my dinghy secured in its usual spot. Three teenage girls were loitering around the dock, and I asked them if they might know who it was that had been stealing my dinghy. Of course they denied any knowledge. I told them that if they did see who it was I'd appreciate their informing them that the next time anyone tampered with it, I would contact the RCMP. This game would continue throughout much of my stay at Alert Bay, but, fortunately, I always had my dink when I needed it.

Since visiting Billy Proctor's museum, I'd been interested in Indian trading beads. These simple, rough, glass beads had been used as a commodity back in the days of European exploration and settlement of the Americas. Often vast tracts of land were traded for a handful of beads. Explorers and settlers took advantage of the fact that native inhabitants did not understand the concept of land ownership; they belonged to the Earth, the Earth did not belong to them. Indians thought they were getting a great deal because they were trading something that was not theirs for something of value.

Many of these beads found their way into middens and the ruins of settlements, where sometimes they become exposed by the elements. Since digging up middens without a special permit has been banned, the likelihood of finding trading beads has greatly diminished. It was my hope to acquire some along the way as a keepsake.

My search led me to Guy, an Indian by blood who was not recognized as having tribal status by the Canadian government. Thus Guy was denied the benefits to which treaty tribes were entitled. He was physically challenged and eked out a modest living as best he could by selling his carvings and paintings. Guy had managed to find a number of beads over the years. He treasured the beads as part of his heritage, yet expressed a willingness to sell me a couple for only ten dollars each! Why would he be willing to part with a personal treasure for so little? He needed cigarettes and beer. Such is the lot of those fighting addictions, a plight all too common among the native people of our continent. I could not in good conscience take the beads under those circumstances, so I declined his offer and instead offered to buy him his beer and smokes. Later, as I bid him farewell and prepared to take my leave he placed the beads in my hand as a gift. I resolved to someday fashion a necklace around those beads to forever remind me of my visit to Alert Bay.

I was to end up spending a month and a half in and around Alert Bay as I waited to conclude the land purchase. Ultimately, the deal was to fizzle out. It seems that the land was under review for inclusion in a "development permit zone," which did not mean it couldn't be built on, but that it would be difficult and costly. This was a piece of vital information that Steven had neglected to share with me. My instincts had been telling me to be cautious, but I had proceeded anyway. When I found out that the land was in a potential slide zone, my reservations were validated. It was with a heavy heart that I withdrew from the deal. As I said earlier, I feel that a handshake is as binding as a signature on a contract, so I really had to search my soul to see if I could back out with a clear conscience, as my integrity is very important to me. I felt that the failure to share vital information about the land justified my decision not to go forward with the purchase, and my deposit was returned.

All in all my stay in Alert Bay had proven a highlight of my journey. I'd met many interesting people and experienced many new things. I also had learned some lessons.

Chapter Nineteen

Throughout my stay in Alert Bay, I'd often heard of a man called "Walrus" who was of some notoriety. Walrus Oakenbough was a pen name adopted by David Garrick when he was writing a column for a Vancouver newspaper.

In the early 1970s Garrick had been one of the key people in Greenpeace, at a time when Greenpeace was among the world's foremost environmental activist groups. It was a time of growing awareness that the world was not a limitless resource to be exploited and plundered without thought for the future. Greenpeace had pioneered a method of protecting endangered whales from slaughter, by physically placing themselves between whaling ships (with their harpoon cannons) and their defenseless victims. Greenpeace members did this on the high seas, in small inflatable boats deployed from their mother-ship, the *Rainbow Warrior*.

Rainbow Warrior was also used to obstruct nuclear bomb tests being carried out by the French on a Pacific atoll. Walrus was present when the French navy sent frogmen equipped with magnetic limpet mines to sink the *Rainbow Warrior*, at a cost of one life. The perpetrators were charged and convicted of murder but were given over to the custody of the French government, which promptly released them.

Walrus was also involved in Greenpeace's Labrador project, in which they spray-painted harp seal pups in order to render their pelts useless to the hunters who would club the pups to death and skin them on the ice, only to leave their corpses to the elements. Often they would skin the defenseless creatures alive, to the horror of any human with a shred of decency. The thought of such barbaric behavior is sickening. A photo of one of these snow-white pups, with their shiny black eyes, will often bring sighs of adoration. It's beyond comprehension to imagine one writhing in agony, awash with blood. Walrus had been an important man in a significant organization with a worthy cause.

I met the notorious Walrus in Alert Bay, where he was a regular visitor. He had the appearance of a genuine early ~~American~~ Canadian hippie. The day I met him, he was in need of transportation back to his camp on nearby Hanson Island. I offered him a lift aboard *Pato*. As luck would have it, Paul Spong, his friend and compatriot from Greenpeace days, was able to give him a ride. (Paul continues to be involved in whale conservation. He operates Orca Lab on Hanson Island, where he studies the creatures.) Walrus had been grateful for my offer of transportation and invited me to visit his camp anytime.

Sunday, July 8 I made my first attempt to locate Walrus' camp. I motored up the south side of the Pierce Islands and through a narrow channel between the Plumper Islands and Hanson Island before making my way into a cove where I dropped the hook. I rowed ashore and found a trailhead, which ultimately led me nowhere.

The next day I returned to Alert Bay, where contrary to the nature of the human male, I sought out directions on how to find the right trail.

Friday, July 14 With a little more information in hand, I set out again for Hanson Island. This time I anchored in Dong Chong Bay, the easternmost of several bays and coves along the island's southern shore. I soon found the trail that would eventually lead me to Walrus' camp.

After a short hike through the forest I encountered a rustic gate. I let myself in and closed the gate behind me. I called out, "Hello in the camp!" so as not to startle anyone. Walrus responded with the Kwak'wala greeting of "Yo!" We shook hands and he invited me to tour his camp and meet his son, daughter, and their friend, all of whom were visiting.

The camp consisted of a couple tents and a number of shacks, constructed by hand of materials gathered from the forest and shore. The entire compound was surrounded by a fence of salal branches woven into the surrounding brush. (The fence was needed to keep marauding deer from decimating Walrus' gardens.) Walrus had hacked out several small garden plots from the forest, and he raised a number of native plants alongside vegetables you might find in a suburban garden. The soil had been enriched as a result of a huge fire that had swept over Hanson Island some four hundred years ago and turned the thick duff of the ancient forest floor into ash. The camp's drinking water was carried by bucket from a small stream a short distance away, and a latrine was used to answer the call of nature. The overall impression was that someone had come to spend a few weeks camping in the woods and had stayed for years.

Having toured the camp, Walrus and I settled in to get acquainted over coffee. He had indeed been living more or less full-time in this camp for about twenty years. Walrus is an archeologist specializing in the study of local cultures. He also has a fascination with the ancient Mayan civilization, and for many years he has maintained a journal which follows the Mayan calendar. He showed me his journal, and I found it fascinating as well as beautiful, with its brightly colored hieroglyphic symbols.

Walrus has studied and documented thousands of "culturally modified trees," or "CMTs," throughout the thick forest of the island. CMTs are trees that have been modified by harvesting bark and lumber from live trees. The native people hack a notch in the bark about a third of the way around the trunk, and then pull the bark away from the trunk. The bark comes off in a long tapering strip extending high up on the trunk, leaving a distinctive scar on the tree. Studies have shown that trees that have had bark harvested actually generate more bark surface than unmodified trees as the surrounding bark grows around the scar. Several years or perhaps a generation later, the people would again harvest bark from the tree, from another side. The bark was used for clothing, shelter, art, and even food. Another use of the trees was to remove planks of lumber from the living tree by hacking two notches in the trunk of the tree, one above the other and then prying the lumber out from between the two notches. This practice was carried on by generation after generation of First Nations people for as long as the tree lived. Some of the trees Walrus has studied have had as many as six bark harvests performed.

The "Grandmother Cedar," a western red cedar on Hanson Island, is approximately 1,400 years old and has survived many such harvests. The tree is about sixteen feet in diameter at the butt and still lives today. It is a magnificent example of the type of tree that once flourished in the Pacific Northwest's temperate forests. There are those who would destroy this tree, justifying their actions by stating how many homes could be built from its lumber, how many jobs it would generate, and how much money its destruction could create. They see this wonder of nature not as a tree but as timber. It is my hope that someday I can show my children or their children this tree; that they can stand in awe of its grandeur. If trees like this are destroyed, never again will we see another like it take its place. The homes constructed of its lumber will have collapsed and been forgotten in a fraction of the time it has taken this tree to reach this age.

The native practice of harvesting material from the trees while allowing it to live and grow is a model of sustainable use. While it would be impractical to harvest enough timber in this manner to meet today's demand, we could learn from their example and seek other ways to use the bounty of nature without destroying it.

As a direct result of his studies, which proved a native presence on the island extending back hundreds of years, Walrus was able to thwart an intended logging operation that would have left the island nearly bare of trees. His actions have earned him the undying gratitude of the native people of the area and the disdain of those in the lumber industry.

I learned that Walrus' guests were due to depart the next day and again offered to provide transport. They were glad to accept.

Saturday, July 15 I ferried my passengers two at a time out to *Pato* in my dinghy and weighed anchor at 0900 hours for Alert Bay. The sky was mostly sunny and winds calm, and we all had a nice visit as we motored. I dropped Yuki, Ryosuke, and Manna at the marina adjacent to the ferry dock in plenty of time for them to catch the next ferry to Port McNeill. After Walrus and I saw them off, we grabbed a few provisions and set out again for Hanson Island. We attempted to power through a narrow cut in the Plumper Islands but were forced to wait for the turn of the tide, as the current was too strong to overcome. Walrus directed me into a snug little cove in one of the islands, where we anchored to pass the time. As we wiled away the hours, we had a wonderful conversation. When the tide turned, we weighed anchor and made our way back to Dong Chong Bay, where we dropped the hook at 1800 hours. We agreed to get together in the morning for coffee. I rowed Walrus ashore and returned to *Pato* for the night.

With my efforts to buy land in Alert Bay temporarily delayed, I had time to kill. I asked Walrus if I could be of any help around his camp as a volunteer. When I had served as a volunteer with the Sailing Heritage Society, I had found the experience very rewarding. My work with the society had in fact led me to *Pato*, the vessel which had carried me to this place.

One of the shacks in Walrus' camp served as a library, office, and living room. Some time ago, an addition had been begun but not finished. The walls had been framed with poles gathered from the forest, and a few rafters had been set. The rafters were naturally curved logs, which added a lot of character to the structure. This was just the kind of project I could get into. When I'd had my cabin on Herron Island, I'd built a tree house and barn using mostly salvaged material. The skills I acquired there would serve me well on a project like this.

Walrus gladly accepted my offer to pick up where the previous craftsman had left off. We set out into the forest to find the materials we would need. Over the next couple of days we found enough curved logs to finish the rafters, and I set about crafting and setting the remaining rafters. Working in logs, let alone curved logs, is a whole different discipline than working in dimensional lumber and poses many challenges. When I build something I like to make it beautiful, and this was a great opportunity to build something unique while I polished my construction skills for future projects on the land I intended to buy in Alert Bay. As more rafters were added, the gambrel roof began to take on the appearance of a boat being built upside-down. Walrus and I joked that when the time came, it could serve as an ark.

Wednesday, July 19 I set out again for Alert Bay at 1330 hours to pick up Manna and her fiancé, Dan, and give them a ride to Hanson Island. They were due to arrive on Friday, but I headed back early in order to buy provisions and rest my aching body. It had been months since I'd swung a whammer (hammer) and I could really feel it. The sky was overcast and the wind calm, so I just motored.

As I passed between the Pierce Islands and the Plumper Islands, I spotted a pod of Dall's porpoises about the same time they detected my presence. They came charging over to frolic on my bow wave and accompanied me through the passage.

I dropped the hook in Alert Bay at 1545 hours and kicked back for the evening. I spent a couple days checking on the progress of the land purchase, buying provisions, and checking in with Steven, Judy, and my other new friends.

Friday, July 21 I met Manna and Dan at the marina and we set out for Hanson Island. It was a beautiful day with clear, sunny skies and a northwesterly breeze of only five knots. We motored down Broughton Channel and through the Blow Hole at slack water before continuing east along Blackfish Sound. As I started my turn into Dong Chong Bay, we spotted a pod of orcas to the east, and I changed course in order to enjoy the show. We observed the pod from a distance of about a half mile. When the orcas drew away to the west, we made our way into the bay and dropped the hook at 2100 hours. I rowed my guests ashore and returned to *Pato* to enjoy a spectacular sunset.

Not long before my journey had begun, an orca calf was discovered alone near Fox Island in the south Puget Sound. The local TV stations got wind of it and dispatched helicopters to obtain aerial footage for their broadcasts. I recall seeing film of the calf, whom the media dubbed "Springer," pursuing a salmon that appeared much too large for him to tackle. Clearly, Springer was much too young to fend for himself, and soon a plan was afoot to reunite him with his pod. He had been captured and transported to the very spot where I chose to anchor in Dong Chong Bay. This spot had been chosen due to the fact that nearly every year the resident pods of orca that frequent the inland coastal waters congregate to form a "superpod" in this vicinity. Perhaps superpods are to orcas what the potlatch had been to the native people. The identity of Springer's pod was never in question due to the fact that each pod is studied and identifying marks catalogued from birth. When Springer's pod arrived near the bay, he was released, and he was soon back in the midst of his kin.

Saturday, July 22 I weighed anchor and set out for the small cove in the Plumper Islands that Walrus had shown me. I needed to spend some time completely alone to mull over what to do about the land deal.

Along the way, my attention was drawn to something splashing off my starboard bow. It wasn't the type of splash one would expect to see from a fish, seal, or sea-lion. Closer inspection by binoculars revealed nothing. As I approached the spot, it became apparent that it was a bald eagle that had caught a fish too large for his ability to take wing. The eagle was doing his version of the butterfly stroke as he swam ashore with his catch. Eventually, he found shore and clambered up onto the rocks to feast on his salmon.

After the eagle's performance, I made my way into the cove and dropped the hook. I sunbathed on deck for a while before rowing ashore and exploring the whole island naked. I feel that there is something magical about communing with nature in our natural state. I have never been to a nudist camp and have no interest in doing so; I simply enjoy the feel of the sun's warmth or the coolness of water against my bare skin.

That evening, I had a fire on the beach before turning in for the night. In the morning, I hung out for a while before my solitude was disturbed by a fleet of charter fishing boats, which descended on my sanctuary intent on having a party and barbeque on the beach.

With my tranquility disrupted, it was time to move on. I weighed anchor and headed for Alert Bay. I'd made my decision not to buy the land. I needed to see Stephen and tell him of my decision. I'd come to realize that there were simply too many warning bells to be ignored. The next day I accomplished this rather painful task, and then I spent a few days performing maintenance and doing minor repairs.

Friday, July 28 I'd come to realize that my body was not going to allow me to continue work on Walrus' library any longer. I weighed anchor and set out for Hanson Island for what would be the last time on this voyage. It was mostly sunny and the northwesterly winds were up to twenty knots. Despite having perfect sailing conditions, I ended up motoring. Emotional turmoil over the land deal had left me a little out of sorts, and I just didn't feel up to the task of sailing.

Along the way, I followed a couple whale watching tour boats to a spot off Stubbs Island, where some humpbacks were feeding on the surface. They were swimming on their sides with their huge mouths agape, scooping immense mouthfuls of water and filtering their catch through their baleens. The show was culminated by one of the whales breeching, throwing itself into the air to twist and fall back into the water with an enormous splash.

I made my way back into Dong Chong Bay, dropping the hook there for the last time. In the morning, I hiked the short distance to Walrus' camp to bid him farewell. He expressed his gratitude for my efforts in continuing the library project and transporting him and his family to and fro. For my part, I was simply grateful for the opportunity to have rubbed elbows with a man who has lived his life by his convictions; a man whose presence on this earth has had a positive impact. Walrus and his compatriots have shown humanity that a small group of dedicated people can help save the world.

A Spot of Legalese

Don't even think about using the "chart" on the adjoining page for navigational purposes! If you do, you're more stupider than me! It is only an illustration provided to distract you from the lack of substance in my words. This may give you an idea of where I went, even if I didn't have a clue where I was going ... Still don't!

The Voyage of Pato Feo

Beware the Sirens

N51°00.00'

British Columbia

Canada

Queen Charlotte Strait

The Braughton Group

Cape Scott

Johnstone Strait

Octopus Islands

Quatsino Sound

Desolation Sound

Princess Louisa Inlet

Brooks Peninsula

N50°00.00'

Vancouver

Copeland Islands

Kyuquot Sound

Espiranza Inlet

Island

Nootka Sound

Howe Sound

Estevan Point

Strait of Georgia

Clayoquot Sound

N°00.00'

Barkley Sound

Here be Dragons

Port San Juan

Strait of Juan de Fuca

Olympic Peninsula

N48°00.00'

N

W

E

S

Puget Sound

Pacific Ocean

Washington State

N47°00.00'

2006

U.S.

W128°00.00'

W127°00.00'

W126°00.00'

W125°00.00'

W124°00.00'

W123°00.00'

Here dwell Pirates

Chapter Twenty

Wednesday, August 2 The time had finally come for me to leave Alert Bay and Hanson Island behind. Once I'd decided that Alert Bay was not to be my home, I'd grown anxious to move on and seek new adventures. I paid the village one more visit so I could fill my water tank and grab some last minute provisions, including just one more ice-cream cone. It was with a heavy heart that I strolled through the village for the final time.

And so at 1500 hours, I cast off the lines and turned *Pato's* bow west toward the end of Vancouver Island. I motored awhile, reflecting on my feelings about my stay in the area I was now leaving in my wake. I concluded that it had been a highlight of highlights, despite the failed land deal and the false signals about Judy. Perhaps one day I would return to the area, but that would be for future adventures. For now, it was time to seek new horizons.

As I motored out of the bay and rounded Yellow Bluff, the village that had nearly become my home disappeared from view. I passed north of Waddington Island and continued west along Broughton Strait. Clearing Pulteney Point on Malcolm Island, I found that the wind had built to a nice northwesterly fifteen knots so I made sail. As I entered Queen Charlotte Strait, the wind built to twenty knots, although it was a little flukey. The wind waves grew to about four feet, which reduced my speed. As I'd gotten a late start, I found it necessary to start the engine and motor-sail in order to reach shelter before dark.

As I continued along the strait, a group of humpbacks followed the same course about a mile ahead. They kept me amused by repeatedly slapping the water with their distinctive pectoral fins, and breaching. It is difficult to say if this behavior is a way of communicating or if they are simply being playful. Since humpbacks are noted for their beautiful vocalizations, which can be heard for many miles underwater and are likely a very effective form of communication, I suspect they were simply having fun.

I considered stopping at Port Hardy, but had begun to feel the need for solitude and did not need any provisions so opted for Beaver Harbor. I handed the sails as I passed by Eagle and Deer Islands before passing between Cattle and Peel Islands. At 2100 hours I tossed out the hook off the eastern shore of the peninsula that separates Beaver Harbor from Port Hardy. Port Hardy is apparently the point beyond which most insurance companies will no longer cover smaller vessels.

As I backed down on the anchor, I noticed a humpback at the far end of the harbor. He gradually made his way over to my part of the harbor, where he went about the business of lunge feeding on the schools of herring which were plentiful in the harbor. The huge beast would form a "bubble net" by circling the school of fish while slowly exhaling a stream of air, which would scare his prey into a concentrated ball of food. He would then lunge up through the middle of the bubble net, his huge mouth agape to scoop up thousands of fish in one gulp. With his tongue, he then squeezed the water out through his baleen plates, which are like huge feathers the whale uses to filter the food from the water before swallowing his meal. Although I'd seen this feeding technique in documentaries on TV, it was thrilling to see it firsthand at close range. This show went on for some time, and the beast often approached to within a few boat lengths of *Pato*. As I prepared my dinner, I could see him out my galley port-light, and when he blew, it sounded as if he was in the boat with me. It was really something!

As I turned in for the night, I contemplated where to wander next. Across Queen Charlotte Sound lay the mainland coast of British Columbia with its myriad channels, bays, coves, and islands. I did not possess the proper charts to continue very much further north, and I was feeling the need to head south. I missed the kids and longed to see them. With their mom away in Iowa, I felt I needed to be closer at hand in case they needed a parent. Just because they were legally adults didn't mean that my job was done.

I was still vacillating between going down the outside, to complete a circumnavigation of Vancouver Island, or returning down the inside.

Although I'd explored much of the inside route, there remained much to be seen if I reversed course down the inside. Outside lay an untapped reserve of sights to be seen and memories to be made.

As a kid, I remembered watching the surf pound on the ocean beaches from ashore and wondering how a small boat could survive the huge waves. I thought of the immense seas I'd seen on TV and recalled harrowing stories of survival by mariners caught in storms.

What kind of conditions could I expect on the outside? More often than not, the weather forecasts for the west coast of Vancouver Island were for gale winds and large seas. Also, I'd heard others refer to the month of August as "fogust," for the heavy fogs which regularly blanket the coast. I had no radar and had to rely only into my GPS to find my way in the fog.

I considered the seaworthiness and condition of my boat. My suit of sails was definitely getting a little ragged; would they survive a real blow? Was *Pato* really suited for ocean sailing? Did I possess the skills needed to face the "big pond"? My only experience on the mighty Pacific Ocean had been the short jaunt up to Barkley Sound a year prior with Daniel, aboard *Vientos de Cambio*, and that had been in flat calm conditions.

What of the hazards to be found out there? There were rocks and currents, fog and storms, not to mention pirates and sirens, serpents, and dragons! Oh no, not dragons!

When navigating, upon reaching the edge of a chart you look for the number of the adjoining chart noted in the margin. I harkened back to the days of discovery when there were no adjoining charts. When they reached the edge of the known world, the charts would often say only "thar be dragons." I came to wonder what had become of those pesky dragons. I concluded they'd been chased off. What could be scary enough to send dragons scurrying off the edge of the earth I wondered? It must have been women. Women have always scared the hell out of me, why wouldn't they scare dragons too? What kind of women, might you ask? I conjured up the image of an extraordinarily fierce race of women that had purged the world of the beasts. They were "psychotic militant premenstrual amazon lesbian pirate-witch vampire-demons with flaming tampon fuses packin' unregistered hand-guns and sportin' tattoos of Charlton Heston." That must be what scared 'em off! (If I've failed to offend anyone, I apologize. Please forward your hate mail to the publisher.)

Intrepid offshore sailors will likely scoff at my fears; after all, this was only coastal sailing. I would never be more than a few hours from shelter. But bear in mind that just a few short years before, I'd been sailing a ten foot dinghy in the sheltered waters of Puget Sound.

As I lay in my bunk that evening, I continued to debate the subject; inside or outside, in or out? At last I made my decision. My decision was to continue my deliberations for another day. It wasn't as if I was procrastinating … well, yea, actually I was.

Thursday, August 3, 1000 hours I weighed anchor and laid a course for Hope Island which would place me north of Vancouver Island and tantalizingly close to the elusive fifty-first parallel. Wherever my wanderings would carry me, at least I could say I'd travelled the length of Vancouver Island.

It was a beautiful day with a northwesterly wind of fifteen to twenty knots and seas of one to two feet. I made sail and beat to weather up Goletas Channel. It was a perfect day for sailing and *Pato* was pointing very well. She was perfectly balanced, and she and I were very much in sync. As usual, the scenery was magnificent as I sailed the length of the channel that separates Vancouver Island from Duncan, Hurst, Balaklava, and Nigei Islands. After a wonderful day of sailing, I handed the sails and made my way into Bull Harbor on Hope Island, where I dropped the hook at 1800 hours. The harbor nearly cuts the island in two. Only a narrow isthmus separates the harbor from the open sea.

Regardless of where I chose to wander next, I'd reached a milestone. I was now north of Vancouver Island. As I made my way into the harbor, I turned the last page of my cruising atlas, which covers the area from Olympia to Queen Charlotte Sound, and opened my next atlas, which covers the west coast of Vancouver Island.

Stay tuned for the next installment in the ongoing saga of Ron's journey through life; a tragic comedy. Some nudity, adult humor and profanity. Viewer discretion is advised.

Part Three
And trust I will not breathe me last

Chapter Twenty-One

Friday, August 4, 2006 Bright sunlight streaming in through the open hatch above my cozy bunk roused me from slumber. My eyes slammed open and another day began. I lay at anchor in Bull Harbor, Hope Island. Some three and a half months had passed since I'd cast off the lines and left my home port. My day started like many others, with a pot of coffee in my bunk, but on this particular morning I didn't read my book. Instead, I pondered once more which direction my travels would take me. The time had come to head toward home.

The question remained, inside or outside? Scattered around me on the bunk were my collection of charts, tide and current tables, and other navigation publications. I listened to the weather forecast predict light to moderate winds and swells for "west coast Vancouver Island, north." A neap tide would reduce the tide rips off Cape Scott and light winds and moderate currents would mean favorable conditions on Nahwitti Bar. I plotted a course and laid out a route in my GPS, to Sea Otter Cove in San Joseph Bay. I chose this destination not for its merit as a cruising ground, but due to the fact that it is the first shelter to be found on the outside. If the weather should deteriorate or those pesky dragons return, I could run and hide there. If I got an early start, I could ride the ebb across the bar, hit Cape Scott at slack water, and ride the flood down the coast. The conditions were as near perfect as one could hope to get.

I considered the fact that having come this far, if I didn't go outside now I might never again have the opportunity. Go or no-go? For days, weeks, and months I'd been delaying the inevitable and deferring the decision for some future date. That date had arrived. After months of deliberation, the decision came down to one brief moment. Let's do it! Outside it is!

With the decision finally made, I simply weighed anchor at 1000 hours, motored out of the harbor, and turned west. As I motored across Nahwitti Bar I encountered long gentle swells. Clearing Cape Sutil, I turned southwest and headed for Cape Scott, standing offshore about a mile.

As I motored along, I could see the rollers breaking on the beach and the odd whale in close ashore. I was blessed again with a bright, warm day, as had been the case for nearly my entire journey. Riding the ebb, I made good time and just as planned, I reached Cape Scott at slack water.

I'd plotted a course which would carry me well clear of the tide rips in Scott Channel, but conditions were so favorable that I cut the corner in order to save a few miles. As I turned southeast toward my destination, the wind began to build. When the northwesterly wind reached twenty knots, I hoisted the main and jib, rigged a preventer and whisker pole to fly wing-n-wing, and ran free before the wind. Too soon I reached my waypoint off Cape Russell near my destination for the day.

With such beautiful conditions, and plenty of daylight remaining, I checked to see if another destination was within reach. About twenty miles further down the coast lay Quatsino Sound, which had much more to offer in terms of cruising than did San Joseph Bay. I chose to forge ahead.

The long, gentle swells and moderate wind waves served as a reminder that I was no longer sailing inland waters, and it felt great! I loved the sensation of sitting in my cockpit (which is perhaps five feet above the waterline) and looking up at the rollers as they approached, lifted *Pato*, then gently lowered her again. I began to feel silly for all of my anxiety about venturing outside.

With wind and current in my favor I was making about seven knots, and soon I was off the mouth of Quatsino Sound. At 1915 hours, I jibed and rounded up into a beam reach which would carry me into the sound. Without the mizzen I had a little lee helm, but it was quite manageable. Had I flown the mizzen, I probably would have been overpowered, and being so close to my destination I didn't want to go to the trouble of shaking it out only to have to douse it again in a few minutes.

Entering Forward Inlet, I handed the sails and proceeded under power. As I made my way into the harbor, I saw the first sea otters of my voyage. There were quite a number of them floating on their backs. They paid little attention to my passing. Sea otters are quite different from the river otters I was accustomed to seeing. They are much larger and have scruffy whiskers. They seemed content to just relax, as if reclining in a lounge chair. River otters seem much more active, like typical adolescents.

I sniffed around for an anchorage by Mathews Island, but the good spots were already taken so I continued a little farther up the inlet. At 2100 hours I dropped anchor near the village of Winter Harbor.

It had been a long day and I was exhausted. All of the deliberations that had finally led to the decision to go outside had been tiring, but it was with a great sense of satisfaction and anticipation that I drifted off into a deep, restful sleep.

Saturday, August 5 I slept in and awoke refreshed and eager to continue my adventure. I became aware that the air had a different feel to it. It felt fresher and cooler, and the smell was definitely that of the sea.

After breakfast, I weighed anchor and motored over to the government dock so I could stretch my legs a bit. After a pleasant walk, I cast off the lines at 1200 hours and set out for Port Alice, which lies near the end of Neroutsos Inlet. I'd heard that there were very cheap houses to be had there, due to the closure of the lumber mill that had been its sole source of employment.

There was a nice northwesterly wind of ten to fifteen knots, so I made sail and sailed a series of broad reaches along the length of the sound. As I passed Drake Island via Buchholz Channel, the wind started to ease.

As I proceeded through the channel, I noticed a beautiful cove in which to anchor. Although I only had about ten miles to go to reach Port Alice, the cove looked too inviting to pass. Besides, the water ahead looked calm, and I thought it safe to assume that Port Alice would still be there tomorrow. I lined up on the narrow entrance to the cove and sailed in to drop the hook under sail at 1700 hours.

Julian Cove is all but landlocked by its narrow entrance; it would be a great place to ride out a storm. After dinner I read for a while and turned in early.

Sunday, August 6 I rose early and lowered the dinghy to explore the cove. A grassy area on the shore beckoned to me, and I rowed there for a walk in the forest, in hopes of finding some mushrooms. Due to the extremely dry season we'd been enjoying there had been few, if any, to be found to date. Here the 'shrooms were finally beginning to fruit, although I didn't find any that I could positively identify as edible.

After my walk, I returned to *Pato* and weighed anchor at 1000 hours to set out once more for Port Alice. Winds were calm, so I proceeded under power to the end of the inlet. Passing close ashore, I looked the town over. For whatever reason, I didn't find it particularly appealing. Nor did I see a convenient place to moor *Pato*, so I headed back down the inlet.

The wind briefly rose to about ten knots, but the water ahead looked flat. I wasn't feeling too ambitious so I didn't bother making sail, opting to troll for a while. I was at last rewarded with a ling cod. I hadn't enjoyed a great deal of success in fishing on this voyage, but then I don't know a great deal about the sport. A couple of years before, when I'd caught my first ling cod I'd had to frantically thumb through the pages of my fishing regulations pamphlet to find a picture of my catch so I could identify what it was! My main interest in fishing is not so much in the fishing, but in the eating! I've never understood the whole catch and release concept, nor do I understand why anyone would want to catch a game fish that isn't palatable. The critter I'd just hauled in was definitely destined to find his way into my belly in the very near future.

Leaving Neroutsos Inlet, I passed between Drake Island and Lindgren Point. I considered exploring Holberg and Rupert Inlets, but the tide was on the ebb and I would be unable to make way against the flow in Quatsino Narrows. Besides the logging activity in the mountains lining the shore held little promise of scenic wonders to be found farther up the inlets.

The wind remained calm as I passed north of Drake Island and continued west back the length of Quatsino Sound. Wishing to position myself for an early exit in the morning, I chose to anchor in Gooding Cove, right at the mouth of the sound. My various publications indicated this was a reasonable anchorage in calm conditions, which were expected. In northwesterly winds, which are the prevailing winds in this region, this would be a lee shore and very exposed to the ocean swells. Gooding Cove would not be the place to be in a blow! I decided to give it a try anyway. At 1800 hours I dropped the anchor in thirty feet of water and settled in for the night.

I sat in the cockpit, smoked my pipe for a while, and kept a wary eye on my position to be sure that the anchor was holding. I could see far out into the Pacific. Long, low swells rolled through the cove to crash on the beach. It was a little un-nerving to be in such an exposed position and I began to question my choice. It was reassuring to read that many others had anchored there before, and I really didn't want to weigh anchor and search for another cove so I decided to stay. I prepared a wonderful meal of fresh ling cod and linguine and called it a night. Although I'd watched carefully to be sure the anchor was holding, I spent a somewhat restless night in my exposed anchorage.

Monday, August 7 I was under way at 0800 hours. Southeasterly winds were forecast and I would be beating to weather. My favorite point of sail is a close reach, but I had not yet had the opportunity to sail *Pato* to weather on the Pacific and didn't know how she would perform. Here was my chance to give it a go.

Ahead lay the Brooks Peninsula, which juts about ten miles out from the coast, perpendicular to the prevailing winds and currents. When listening to weather forecasts on the radio, I'd noted that they often made reference to the hazardous conditions found there. Depending on your position, you could find yourself comfortably sheltered on a weather shore or pummeled by the elements on a lee shore. It is not an area to be trifled with. I hoped to round the peninsula before the winds grew too strong in the afternoon. I plotted a somewhat ambitious course for the day, but I had a Plan "B" and Plan "C" in case conditions deteriorated. (Me and my plans!)

I made sail at the mouth of the cove in ten to fifteen knot winds and enjoyed a nice sail for a while. Soon the wind rose to twenty to twenty-five knots, and with the wind waves against the groundswell my speed was reduced to about three knots. Clearly, my Plan "A" had been too ambitious. I chose to adopt Plan "B," which was Klaskino Inlet. I made my way into the inlet and fetched a mooring buoy by Anchorage Island at 1400 hours. I hadn't made many miles, but better conditions were forecast for the next day, when northwesterly winds of ten to fifteen knots were expected.

With plenty of daylight left, I splashed the dinghy and rowed around a bit. I tried fishing for a while near one of the reefs with my usual success, which is to say none. Later, I rowed ashore to explore the island's beach and woods.

As I beached the dink, I heard a sound not unlike that of a domestic cat. I turned to see a critter about twenty feet away, which I believe was a marten. Its attention was riveted on me and it cautiously approached. It was a little larger than the minks that I'd seen elsewhere in my travels and was somewhat similar in appearance, but had larger, more rounded ears. After he'd had a little closer look at me, and me at him, his curiosity was satiated and he scampered back into the woods. I tried to follow, but the underbrush was nearly impenetrable, so instead I wandered the beach before returning to *Pato* to have dinner and turn in.

Tuesday, August 8 I cast off the mooring line at 0800. It was much easier than having to weigh anchor, but I was less than pleased about the ugly marks the mooring buoy (constructed of old tires) had left on *Pato's* topsides.

It was my intention to round the Brooks Peninsula. A nice northwesterly wind of ten to fifteen knots was expected, so I eagerly anticipated a pleasant day of sailing. As I cleared the inlet, I was greeted with a flat calm. Wind? What wind!? What I got was a whole lot'a too much'a nuthin'. There was not a whisper of a breeze, so I proceeded under power.

As I rounded the peninsula and made my way down the coast, a light fog descended. It had every appearance of thickening. Although I didn't relish the idea of navigating in the fog, I had to be prepared in case I was caught out; after all, it was the month of "fogust." As usual, I'd laid out a route into my GPS. This one would carry me through the rock-strewn entrance of Kyuquot Sound, my destination for the day, should visibility deteriorate. The fog burned off, however, as I continued on my way. Soon I was enjoying another bright, sunny day.

Eventually I had to switch to the reserve fuel tank, as my main tank was getting low. A few hours later, I had a scare when the engine began to sputter as if it were out of fuel. I quickly shut it down before it ran the injectors dry; I did not wish to have to bleed the injectors. I went below to check the fuel gauges, located in the saloon. There I found that the reserve tank, which had been full, was now empty and the main tank, which had been empty, was now full! What gives!?

Fortunately, when I acquired *Pato*, she had come with a complete set of manuals. I recalled seeing a diagram of the fuel system. The system had been designed with a return line only to the main tank. On a diesel engine, you have two fuel pumps; a transfer pump that feeds fuel to the injector pump, which then feeds the injectors. Any fuel pumped to the injectors but unused is pumped back to the tank via the return line. On *Pato*, when using fuel from the reserve tank, the excess fuel is pumped to the main. In only a few hours, I'd pumped all of the fuel out of the reserve and into the main.

I quickly switched back to the main and restarted the engine. It sputtered for a few seconds, as did my heart, before settling back into a smooth rhythm. I was glad that I'd made the decision to stand offshore a mile or so in case something like this happened.

Accompanying me on this leg of my journey was a humpback whale. As we travelled, the leviathan went about his business, and again I was able to observe a whale feeding at close range. As he lunged to the surface with his immense mouth agape, I could see his baleens for a moment before he slammed his mouth shut. The corrugated skin on the underside of his jaw was distended like a huge water balloon before he squeezed out the water and swallowed his prize. Although I'd seen many whales in my travels, I felt a kinship with this particular beast. Often the coast would be obscured by fog, and he would be the only thing visible to me in the void. On one occasion when my friend blew just upwind, I became aware of an offensive odor tainting the salty breeze. I smelled my armpits to see if perhaps I was getting a little ripe. Nope, it wasn't me. Was it my garbage? No, that wasn't it either. Then it dawned on me that what I smelled was whale breath! OK that's carrying kinship a little too far!

Later in the day I saw the first and only puffins of my entire journey. The adorable little birds with their distinctive, colorful bills would dive beneath the waves to resurface with a row of fish held between their upper beaks and tongues. With their catch they took to wing and set out for shore, presumably heading to their nests to feed a clutch of hungry chicks. Their visit had been brief but memorable.

I passed by Nasparti, Ououkinsh, and Malksope Inlets, as well as the Mission Group of the Barrier Islands before entering Kyuquot Sound. I passed southeast of Union Island via Kyuquot Channel, and then turned north to leave Whiteley Island to starboard. Again I turned northeast up Pinnacle Channel to Dixie Cove on Hohoae Island, where I dropped the hook at 1830 hours.

Despite having had to motor for long hours in the calm conditions, it had been another memorable day. As I wound down, I reflected on how I felt about coastal cruising.

Venturing beyond inland waters opened up a world of possible destinations. Oregon and California now seemed tantalizingly close at hand and Mexico not out of reach. From my home waters of the Puget Sound at 48º north, one could sail the coast even as far as Chilean waters at 48º south, where one will find an archipelago rivaling those I'd been exploring these past few months. OK, I might be getting a little carried away! Before I could venture off to the other hemisphere, I needed to safely return to where I'd started. I had to go home.

Fuel System Design

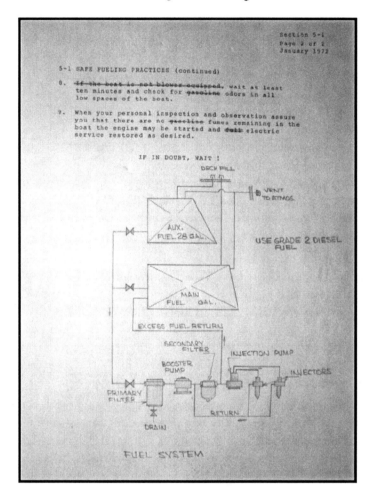

This is yet another diagram done in pencil. It shows that the excess fuel return line goes only to the main tank. This peculiarity of the design gave me a scare off the Pacific coast of Vancouver Island when in a matter of a few hours all of the fuel in the reserve tank was pumped to the main tank, causing the engine to stall.

Chapter Twenty-Two

Wednesday, August 9 I lay at anchor in Kyuquot Sound. A slow, easy morning, nursing a pot of coffee in my comfortable bunk in a deserted cove in the Canadian wilds; a guy could get used to this!

At 0930 hours I weighed anchor and set out to see a little of the sound. The Kyuquot is beautiful, but has only a few inlets and harbors to explore. Also, wherever I wandered, I was pestered by a few very persistent and ravenous horse flies. These critters liked to buzz around until I was distracted, then swoop in to take a bite of fresh meat; my meat! Swatting at them only agitates them and makes them more aggressive. I fashioned a fly swatter from an old magazine and engaged them in combat. For every one that I splattered, it seemed two would take its place!

That morning, I'd been unable to get radio reception in my comfy cove to check the weather report, but as I wandered the sound, I was eventually able to get a radio signal. The forecast was for northwesterly winds of fifteen to twenty knots, building to thirty knots late and forty knots south of the Brooks Peninsula. If I waited too long, I might be pinned down in Kyuquot Sound for some time, and at the rate the horse flies were consuming my flesh, there might not be enough of me left to sail *Pato*.

A short sail away is Esperanza Inlet, which is connected to Tahsis Inlet and Nootka Sound. Heading that direction would allow me to continue my homeward journey along a somewhat sheltered route, and see more of what there was to see of the wilds along the way. At 1330 hours, I fetched the outer buoy and set the main and jib to sail a broad reach down to Esperanza Inlet.

The swells were not large, but the wind waves continued to grow, which made *Pato* a little difficult to handle in the following seas. My attention was focused on steering *Pato*, not on the scenery or wildlife, so I was taken by surprise when about a hundred yards off my starboard bow a humpback suddenly breached! He threw himself in the air and twisted, his pectoral fins spread like wings, then fell back into the sea with an enormous splash. Although I'd seen a few whales breach before, it had never been at such close range. It was a real thrill!

Soon I was off the mouth of Esperanza Inlet. I gibed and sailed into the inlet via Gilliam Channel. My option had been to enter by Rolling Roadstead, but the name alone made me think that wasn't a good choice. (I'd also taken into consideration the numerous rocks and reefs scattered about that entrance.) Just inside the Gilliam Channel entrance were Port Eliza and Queen Cove. I rounded up and sailed through Birthday Channel to a point just outside the cove, where I handed the sails, motored in, and dropped the hook at 1800 hours.

I'd picked Queen Cove partly due to its proximity to the entrance and partly due to the chart's indication that a couple of small lakes might be within walking distance of the cove. It had been a while since I'd bathed and I was beginning to get a little ripe. Fresh water is always a precious commodity when cruising in Canada, even more so in a drought year. I could ill afford to use my limited fresh water for a shower, and the salt chuck here was far too cold for my liking. From my anchorage I could see what appeared to be the mouth of a creek, which I hoped would lead to a lake. I deployed my dinghy and rowed ashore, pausing to drop a crab pot along the way. Once ashore, I followed the dry creek bed into the woods.

The flora in this area was quite different than I had grown accustomed to seeing, consisting mostly of low scrub pines and wild blueberry bushes. Soon the terrain turned steep, and I clambered over rocks up a dry waterfall. Reaching a plateau, I was greeted by the sight of a dry lakebed, or more properly a dry marsh or peat bog. My hopes of a dip in fresh water appeared to be for naught. Oh well, at least I was getting get some exercise. The dry marsh was beautiful, having the appearance of an alpine meadow, so I continued on my way. Walking across the peat produced a rather interesting sensation, like walking across thick, soft, foam rubber. After my walk, I returned to *Pato* and called it a day.

Thursday, August 10, 1100 hours I got under way and paused to retrieve my crab pot before heading up Espiranza Inlet under power. At Steamer Point I turned into Hecate Channel, then continued past the tiny village of Espiranza and through Tahsis Narrows. When I reached Tahsis Inlet, I was greeted by a nice twenty knot southerly wind so I made sail and ran free the short distance to the village of Tahsis, which lies at the end of the inlet. My friend Rick, an avid fisherman, wanted me to check the village out for a possible future fishing trip, and I was about due for fuel, water, and provisions.

As I neared the village, I handed the sails and headed for the marina. I maneuvered toward the fuel dock but was cut off by an angler intent on weighing his catch for the local fishing derby. I was forced to hover in the narrow fairway in the strong flukey wind, until he cleared the dock. Sailboats were very much in the minority amongst the numerous fishing boats. There were a number of anglers waiting at the scale, holding beautiful salmon. After they had weighed in, many would pause for their buddies to take photos before making their way to the cleaning table. It appeared to be a good place for Rick to go on a fishing trip, although it is somewhat remote. To reach Tahsis by road, one must cross Vancouver Island from Campbell River.

There was no sheltered anchorage available, so I decided to spend the night at the dock. After filling my fuel and water tanks, I moved *Pato* to the slip I'd been assigned by the harbormaster, or wharfinger as they used to be called.

Tahsis was the first real village I'd visited since I'd left Alert Bay, so I grabbed my laundry bag and set out in search of a laundromat. Eventually I found one, and while my clothes were washing I wandered about a little. I inquired about where to buy provisions and was directed to the "supermarket" at the other end of town, some distance away. When my clothes were dry, I dropped them off at *Pato*. The wharfinger told me it would be a very long walk to the supermarket, and he kindly offered me the use of a courtesy car.

I hadn't driven a car in several months, so it felt kind of weird at first. I followed the main drag into town and past a rundown convenience store. After driving all over town, or what there was of it, I found myself back at the convenience store, where I finally noticed a weathered old sign touting it as the "supermarket." Inside the supermarket I found mostly bare shelves stocked with a few vintage groceries. I bought some stale cereal and "used bread," as well as a bag of golden raisins as a snack. When I sampled the raisins, they had a rather funny taste; I've heard of dry wine, but I'd never had to chew it! It turns out that the locals have to go across island to Campbell River for their supplies.

The Village of Tahsis is yet another example of a town that was once supported by a lumber mill, now closed. It seems that what remains are mostly vacation and retirement homes, and of course the sport fishing industry.

It had been a while since I'd eaten in a restaurant, so I decided to try the Mexican restaurant at the marina. The food was on par with Taco Bell, which is to say not very good, but at least it was expensive! The best thing I could say about my dining experience was that it produced muy bueno pedos. Hey, gas ain't cheap!

Friday, August 11 I was under way by 0940 hours, eager to leave the hustle-bustle of the dock behind. I made sail as soon as I cleared the dock and flew wing-n-wing on the northerly outflow wind. As I approached Tsowwin Narrows, the wind went calm for a while, so I motor-sailed through the narrows. Coming out the other side, the wind shifted to a southerly inflow and quickly built to twenty to twenty-five knots. With all my canvas aloft and sailing close-hauled, *Pato* was on the verge of being overpowered, but she was still manageable. Next I fell off on a beam reach through Princess Channel and into Kendrick Inlet, where I took a couple of reefs in the main and sailed close-hauled again. Reaching Eliza Passage, I once again fell off and sailed to Valdez Bay in Nootka Sound, where I dropped anchor.

Nootka Sound has more logging activity than I'd previously seen on this voyage, so it was not as pretty as I might have liked. The anchorages were a little on the deep side, but adequate.

Not long before, on the marine weather forecasts, there had been a daily notice to mariners advising that an orphaned orca had taken a liking to playing with sailboat rudders. Orcas, more commonly known as killer whales, can play a little rough, and this one had nearly sunk one sailing vessel that it had used as a chew toy. There had been much talk about what to do with this menace to navigation, but the local First Nations people had come to his defense. The orca, or "blackfish" as some tribes used to refer to them, is one of their spirit animals and thus sacred. Unfortunately he had recently run afoul of a fishing vessel and died, thereby ending the controversy, but not in a manner anyone would have wished.

Chapter Twenty-Three

Since rounding Cape Scott and embarking on the homeward leg of my journey, I'd been enjoying the tranquility to be found on the outside, the road less travelled. The wildlife was wonderful and the scenery spectacular, but no one place had really stood out as a destination. Just down the coast from where I lay was a true destination, Hot Springs Cove.

Saturday, August 12, 0830 hours I weighed anchor and motored out of Nootka Sound on the last of the ebb tide. I ducked through Fidalgo Passage then passed between Nootka Island and the Spanish Group. I tried my hand at trolling for salmon as I slowly made my way out of the sound. As usual, where I was, the fish weren't, or if I was using a green lure they were biting red. In any case, no fish found their way onto my dinner plate.

When I reached open water, the wind rose to about ten knots, so I made sail and set out on a broad reach due south along the shore of the Hesquiat Peninsula.

Rounding Estevan Point, I bid farewell to the area referred to as "west coast Vancouver Island, north." I'd reached yet another milestone. From this point on, when I turned on the VHF radio to listen to the weather forecast, I would be listening for conditions on "west coast Vancouver Island, south."

When I cleared Estevan Point, I fell off to run free before the wind, which had built to a nice fifteen knots with moderate swells. I was then sailing due east and straight toward Hot Springs Cove. At the mouth of the cove, I rounded up and sailed a close reach in through the entrance. I ghosted along the rocky shore and past the government dock to a notch in the cove's shore, where I dropped the hook at 1900 hours. I handed the sails and jumped in the dinghy to row over to the dock. I was eager to see the hot springs and have a soak.

At the head of the dock I found a signboard stating that nude bathing was prohibited. What!? One of the best things about soaking in Mother Nature's own hot tub is doing it as we were made! It is generally accepted that clothing is optional at most hot springs, so I was a little surprised and disappointed that a bathing suit was required here. Fortunately, I'd brought mine ashore with me.

The signboard also had a collection box for a day use fee to use the hot springs. At first I was taken aback at the notion of having to pay to use something that Mother Nature had blessed us with, but that was soon forgotten as I set out on the boardwalk leading off into the woods and to the springs.

The boardwalk was beautifully constructed of rough-cut cedar and followed the natural contours of the forest floor, over, under, and around the obstacles left by nature. At every curve or corner in the walk, the craftsmen who constructed it had lovingly cut the planks to craft a beautiful fan-shaped pattern. They could have simply cut abrupt angles and built a very serviceable boardwalk, but they had opted to make it something beautiful. I felt a little sheepish about having objected to the fee when I found what it would be used to support. I set out down the boardwalk with a vengeance, hoping to reach the springs before nightfall.

Along the way I began to encounter planks in which yachties had carved the name of their boats along with their hailing port, and often the date, and sometimes the names of their crew. At first I was a little surprised to see that defacing the walk would be tolerated, but soon I came to realize that it was in fact encouraged. This was not vandalism, but more a way of carrying on a longstanding tradition among mariners of leaving their mark at various destinations. Many harbors around the world have walls or rocks adorned with similar messages, some dating back hundreds of years. Along this walk were hundreds of carvings, some beautifully crafted and others mere scratches. Nowhere did I see any signs of profanity or malicious vandalism. Aboard *Pato*, I happened to have a set of carving tools perfectly suited to this type of carving and I resolved that I too would leave my mark.

The path carried me over and under fallen trees and through groves of old-growth cedars. After an invigorating walk, I crossed a bridge over a small, steaming creek, turned a corner, and arrived at the springs.

The hot springs emerge from the earth a few steps from the bridge I'd just crossed, at which point, the water is scalding hot. It flows a short distance to a series of shallow pools in the solid granite, where it cools slightly before cascading over a small waterfall that forms a natural shower. The rivulets that had the higher flow and had taken the shortest path were quite hot but tolerable, others were a little cooler. The water then flows through a series of natural pools in the granite, growing progressively cooler with each successive pool before eventually finding its way to the sea. From the lower pools, one can see across the cove and far out into the Pacific. At higher tides these lower pools are flooded with sea water; at times it is possible to have waves crashing into your pool as you soak. Some of the pools are large enough to accommodate several people; others are smaller and more intimate. The bottoms of the pools are covered with a nice bed of gravel that is kind to bare feet. There is almost no sulfur smell, the water is clear, and there is little algae or microbial growth. One could scarcely imagine a more idyllic setting.

I quickly changed into my bathing suit and lowered myself into the first pool. It was a little too hot at first, so I moved on to the next pool and the next until I found one of a suitable temperature. Once acclimatized, I was able to move back to the hotter pools. I shared the pools with a few other bathers, but it was not crowded. I learned that after nightfall the no nude bathing rule was generally ignored. After a while I stood under the waterfall and let hot water massage my body, which was still suffering the effects of my overexertion on Hanson Island. The heavy pounding of the hot water had the desired effect, and soon my aches and pains were greatly diminished. I felt rejuvenated and clean as I made my way back along the boardwalk to the dock. Returning to *Pato*, I had a bite and turned in.

The next morning, I was nursing a pot of coffee in the cockpit when a seaplane swooped low over the cove, turned, passed close at hand at masthead height, and landed a short distance away. He taxied over to the dock, where his passengers disembarked. He departed for another load while another plane landed. Soon after the planes left, tourist boats began to arrive.

I thought that it might be better to wait until later in the day to enjoy another soak, so instead I grabbed my carving tools, intent on marking my passage on the boardwalk. I brought along the proof of the script I'd used when ordering the lettering adorning *Pato*'s transom; I could duplicate the script so that my mark on the boardwalk would match that found on *Pato*. I selected a board not far up the path and went about the business of carving. My dad had been an avid wood carver, and I feel he would have been proud of my efforts. If you visit Hot Springs Cove, you will now find a plank with the inscription "*Pato Feo*, Tacoma, WA '06."

As I was putting the finishing touches on my carving, a young man who had been observing my actions struck up a conversation. Brandon was fourteen years old and was travelling with his mother and stepfather aboard their thirty-eight foot sloop. While we chatted, he juggled a few stones with the skill you would expect of a circus performer. He told me he also is able to perform while riding a unicycle. Of greater interest to me was a necklace he wore, crafted of twine and featuring a number of intricate knots. It had a very nautical flair and was a prime example of marlinspike seamanship. I asked Brandon where he had acquired it, and was surprised when he told me he'd made it himself.

With my carving complete, I set out for the springs. Brandon accompanied me and we continued our chat along the way. Tying intricate knots is a hobby he likes to practice while under way, but unfortunately he had exhausted his supply of raw material. I had a large supply of line I thought he might find suitable and I told him we might be able to work out a trade. I would give him a quantity of the line in exchange for him crafting a necklace for me, incorporating the trading beads I'd been gifted in Alert Bay.

After a thorough soak, we walked back to the dock and jumped in my dinghy to row out and meet his family. We paused on the way to retrieve the line and let Brandon have a tour of *Pato*; it seems we mariners never tire of looking at boats. He was more than pleased with the quality and quantity of line I offered, and we rowed over to his parents' boat where, after introductions, he set about crafting the necklace. He asked me to select various knots and braids from a book, and then demonstrated some of his favorite knots. In a short while, he'd completed his work and I donned the finished necklace.

As I said my thanks and prepared to take my leave, Brandon offered me the book he'd used to learn his skill. At first I was reluctant, but he assured me he had many such books and besides he'd already mastered every knot in the book! I gratefully accepted and offered my thanks. I would soon put the book to good use.

I spent a few days relaxing at Hot Springs Cove. Of course I took many a dip in the springs, often at night. I also wandered the woods and eventually found my way across the Openit Peninsula to a nice sandy beach where I could sunbathe in private. Although the springs were not crowded, I sought greater solitude. Just across Hot Springs Cove from the government dock is a First Nations reserve and village. I never did venture across, having no great desire for civilization.

Throughout my travels, I'd stayed in touch with Daniel, and we had decided it would be fun to meet somewhere along the way. I decided that this would be a perfect place to hook up. It was Daniel that had introduced me to hot springs and not far from here we had shared our first adventure on the Pacific. I was eager to contact Daniel with my idea, but as there was no cell phone signal in the cove, I would have to move on in search of a signal. Besides, I needed to check in with Jason and Nicole to see how they were doing and let them know all was well with me. With that I prepared to leave Hot Springs Cove behind, for the time being.

Chapter Twenty-Four

Tuesday, August 15, 1000 hours I weighed anchor and motored out of Hot Springs Cove. At the mouth of the cove, I turned 180° around the aptly named Sharp Point and headed due north along Openit Peninsula's shoreline, where I could see the beaches I had enjoyed sunbathing on the past few days. Although the wind rose to a nice ten knots, I continued under power as I needed to fetch Tofino for provisions, water, and hopefully a cell phone signal. At Starling Point, I turned to starboard and followed the shore of Flores Island, passing through Hayden Passage and down Millar Channel.

As usual, the scenery was spectacular: beautiful mountains, endless forests, miles of untouched rocky shoreline with occasional sandy beaches, and the blue, blue water in which I traveled. I'd enjoyed scenic beauty every day on this journey, and had made few references to it in my log and notes. It wasn't that I'd grown jaded to nature's wonders; I constantly admired them. It was that I found myself using the same superlatives to describe sights all along the way.

Eventually I entered an area of shoals that continued as far as Tofino. Navigating these required a degree of concentration. The channels and passages were well marked, but if you missed a turn you could easily find yourself aground. Fortunately, I'd plotted my course and entered a route on my GPS, which greatly simplified my task. I passed north of Vargas Island via Calmus Passage, then down Maurus Channel between Vargas and Meares Islands. With Tofino in sight, the navigation became even more technical. I was constrained to a narrow, dredged channel that wove its way through the shoals. Countless whale watching tour boats, pleasure craft, and work boats zoomed about. Innumerable crab pots flanked the channel, looking as likely to ensnare the unwary mariner as they were their intended prey.

When I reached Tofino, the government dock was filled to capacity, so I continued on to the city-operated marina, where I made *Pato* fast in a vacant slip. When I was finally able to find the wharfinger, I inquired about short-term moorage and availability of potable water. I was directed to move *Pato* to a place near the dock's head, where I could use a metered water spigot that took quarters; lots of quarters. When my water tank was full and my piggy-bank nearly empty, I moved *Pato* to another spot, where I had to fight the strong current to bring *Pato* alongside. I was then exposed to the wake of every passing boat that ignored the no wake zone, which is to say all of them.

I set out on foot with a bag of laundry and soon found a full-service laundromat. While my clothes were being laundered, I stepped next door for a much-needed haircut. Soon the young stylist was running his fingers through my hair in a manner that left little doubt in my mind as to his sexual orientation. Freshly shorn of my locks, I collected my clean clothes and dropped them at *Pato* before setting out again, in search of a grocery store.

Traversing Tofino's sidewalks reminded me of navigating the town's approach channels; out there it had been boats I had to avoid hitting, here it was people. Couples were strolling the sidewalks side by side, completely oblivious of other pedestrians. Often I was forced to step into the street and risk being run down by the cars careening through town. I arrived at a grocery store feeling like I'd run another gauntlet. I procured my provisions and headed back to the dock with a heavy load of groceries and a much lighter wallet, eager to leave this madhouse behind.

Before leaving the dock, I was able to make my phone calls. When I contacted the kids, I was disturbed to learn that Peewee had returned from Iowa and again taken to the bottle. I had hoped that she would find the strength to fight her demons with the help of her mother, a very strong-willed woman. The upsetting truth was that Peewee craved the comfort of drinking regardless of the toll it was taking on her life. No one but her could make the choice for her to quit, no matter how strong their resolve. Chronic alcoholism is an ugly, ugly affliction.

I also contacted Daniel, and we began making our rendezvous plans. It would be a few weeks before he could escape the employment trap, so I would have to cool my heels. Damn, what could I do to kill time? Let's see, I was in an area with many beautiful waterways and islands yet to explore, in a boat that was also my home. Oh, what to do?! Well, I guess I'd just need to find a way to endure! Poor me!

Even though the hour was growing late and the tide on the ebb, I tossed off the lines and got the hell out of town. It was a struggle to motor against the strong current in Browning Passage but eventually I made it through. As the sun began to set, I missed a turn and nearly went aground on a shoal by Indian Island. After I'd collected myself, I ducked into the first cove that resembled an acceptable anchorage and tossed out the hook at 2130 hours, just as darkness fell. It had been an exhausting day, and I was really glad to slam my head onto my pillow and call it a night.

Wednesday, August 16 I arose to see what kind of cove I'd anchored in. It had been nearly dark when I'd arrived, so I didn't know what to expect. The shore was rocky and steep, and I saw little reason to go ashore. Instead, I lolled around the cockpit for a while, reading, and drinking another pot of coffee before getting under way at 1200 hours.

I motored slowly up Tofino Inlet, trolling for whatever might take a liking to my hook and finally rewarded with a small rockfish. I set about the business of filleting my catch with the same level of skill I'd used to catch him, and produced a couple of mangled fillets, which amounted to little more than a mouthful.

Veering to port, I traveled to the head of Tranquil Inlet, simply enjoying the scenery. The breeze began to freshen, so I made sail close-hauled, out of the Inlet. When I reached the end of the McCaw Peninsula, I fell off into a broad reach that carried me to Deer Bay at the head of Tofino Inlet. Where Tofino Creek empties into Deer Bay, its sediment has created a broad shoal area, so I doubled back to the lee of a small island, where I dropped the hook at 1800 hours.

I prepared my dinner, which incorporated my rockfish morsels, and relaxed in the cockpit. Close at hand was a rocky island with gnarled trees leaning out over the water. Across a narrow channel was a sandy beach with a grassy area. All around were jagged mountains, forests extending well up their flanks.

Thursday, August 17, 1100 hours I got under way and set sail out of Deer Bay and Tofino Inlet. The wind was light, but I was in no hurry, so I slowly beat to weather until I reached Indian Island. I fell off and sailed a broad reach up to Dawley Passage, where I jibed and slowly ghosted through. Emerging from the passage, I again jibed and headed north along the shore of Meares Island, toward Mosquito Harbor. Outside of Mosquito Harbor, I spotted an open cove protected by a small island, which just looked too inviting to pass up. There were sandy beaches, and its moderately sloping terrain held promise of a hike. I sailed in and set the hook.

I had an early dinner and rowed ashore to check out the beach. I was not disappointed. The warm sand felt wonderful under my bare feet. The view from shore was breathtaking, *Pato* lying peacefully at anchor next to a small unnamed island, with Fortune Channel in the near background and beautiful mountains in the distance.

The day was very warm and sunny, so I stripped and took a refreshing dip in the salt chuck. As I was waded out to deeper water, each step in the sand released a stream of bubbles that rose to the surface. The effect was like wading in a pool of champagne, and the fizzy bubbles tickled my legs and my fun stuff on the way to the surface. I don't know what it was that caused the air or gas to be trapped in the sand, but the effect was rather interesting.

After swimming, I walked along the beach until I reached a rocky area; being barefoot, I turned back. Returning to the place where I'd come ashore, I donned my clothes and shoes and set out into the forest.

As is often the case, it was difficult to penetrate the forest's perimeter due to thick brush, but once through the barrier it was quite easy to move about. There, the trees blocked much of the light from reaching the forest floor and the undergrowth was sparse. I walked due west up a steep hill, through groves of huge Douglas fir, hemlock and Sitka spruce. The silence in the thick forest was deafening; my breath the only sound. The thick duff of the forest floor was like a carpet beneath my feet.

Meares Island had been another battleground in a modern logging war. First Nations people had claimed aboriginal rights over the island and thwarted plans to strip the island of its timber. Here, as on Hanson Island, culturally modified trees had been used as evidence to support their claims.

North America was once blanketed with rich forests. Only isolated pockets of old-growth forests remain, and they are under constant threat due to economic pressure. The timber industry would have us believe that clear-cutting is better for the forest. Granted, trees grow much faster in an area that has been clear-cut and replanted, and modern tree farms can be easily logged with mechanized harvesting equipment, but what we are losing are forests rich in biodiversity, and what we are substituting is a monoculture. Destroying diversity introduces enormous risks to life as we know it on Planet Earth.

It could be argued that I am a "tree hugger" but I don't just hug 'em! Some might even say that I'm a "tree humper", and these allegations, while not altogether unsubstantiated, have never been conclusively proven and I've destroyed the photographic (pornographic?) evidence.

I was so taken with my surroundings that I chose to stand down and stay at Meares Island another day. I wiled away time enjoying the beach, water, and forest. I saw an occasional boat pass, well out in the channel, but it felt like the world was mine alone.

Saturday, August 19 I enjoyed a leisurely morning on the beach before weighing anchor at 1230 hours. With no particular destination in mind, I trolled awhile and was rewarded with a small salmon. (Or maybe it was a large herring.) The wind began to build, and when it eventually reached fifteen knots I made sail and headed north up Fortune Channel on a broad reach. Turning to port, I jibed and headed west through Matlset Narrows on a close reach. The narrows' flukey winds forced me to motor-sail, but once through, the wind settled, and I headed north up Bedwell Sound on a broad reach. When the wind lightened, I handed the sails and made my way into a conveniently located cove, where I anchored at 1630 hours.

Sunday, August 20 I spent the morning and early afternoon studying the book Brandon had given me and teaching myself the basics of marlinspike seamanship. I was soon tying Turk's Heads, which are intricate decorative knots originally tied by bored seamen long ago.

The wind began to rise, so at 1400 hours, I weighed anchor and made sail. I sailed right off the hook and turned *Pato*'s bow north up Bedwell Sound on a broad reach. The wind grew to twenty-five knots, and *Pato* flew up the sound making seven knots. Too soon, I reached the end of Bedwell Sound and jibed, rounded up, and began beating my way back down the sound. Sailing close-hauled, *Pato* was a little overpowered, and I probably should have reefed the main, but she was pointing well (with perhaps a little too much heeling and weather helm). She wasn't trying to round up on me, so I let her have her reigns, pressing on under a full main. This was sailing at its exhilarating best. The weather was clear and hot, so I was sailin' naked, workin' on me tan. Rounding Rant Point, I turned west and soon reached Cypress Bay. There the wind became flukey, so I handed the sails and made my way to a spot near Rhodes Island, where I tossed out the hook.

Monday, August 21 I lay around the cockpit practicing more knot tying, then began the process of wrapping the helm with nylon line. I chose the ringbolt hitch, which uses three lines and would produce a fairly smooth yet "grippy" surface on the wheel's outside perimeter and a decorative braid around the inside. Using 1/16-inch line would make it a long process, but I felt the results would be worth the effort. At 1400 hours, I finished the first segment of the wheel, leaving only five more to go! It had taken me more than half the day to complete one sixth of the project. I could afford to spend the time, since I was awaiting Daniel's arrival, but my hands and fingers were already feeling the effects of tightening hundreds of hitches. I began to question my sanity for embarking on this project, but perhaps the skill I was developing would serve me well in the "funny farm" in lieu of basket weaving.

My project at a convenient stopping point, I weighed anchor and motored through nearby Quait Bay. Its narrow entrance opens to a nice, sheltered bay with a couple of snug coves. The shore is devoid of development save for a resort, featuring a huge floating hotel and restaurant complex. No signs of activity appeared at the resort, so it would seem that ambitious venture had come to naught.

I motored back out and made sail just outside Quait Bay's entrance. The wind was a beautiful fifteen knots. Across Cypress Bay lay a fog bank, but it began to dissipate as I approached. I had a pleasant sail across the bay and past a few islands, then rounded

Roberts Point and continued down Maurus Channel. Upon reaching Heynen Channel, I'd circumnavigated Meares Island.

I was once again in sight of Tofino and in the clutches of its surrounding shoals, so I handed the sails and motored up Lemmens Inlet to Adventure Cove, where I anchored at 1900 hours. Adventure Cove is thought to have been the site where early explorers had built a ship in order to continue their adventures in the wilds of North America's west coast, although no signs remain of their endeavors. Currently the cove is home to a couple floating houses, where a few families make their homes. This type of home is often found in these waters, and appears to be a wonderful way of life. Unfortunately, this lifestyle is not tolerated in U.S. waters. You have to venture north to see this type of home.

I rowed out, set my crab pot, then continued to shore. I set out on a trail to get some exercise, but I soon lost the trail in an area that had suffered a landslide. Darkness would soon be falling, so I returned to *Pato*.

Wednesday, August 23 At 1000 hours I collected my crab pot, which contained a couple of nice Dungeness, and then set out for Tofino. I needed to visit the madhouse once more to gather a few provisions I'd forgotten in my haste to escape.

Maybe I'm just a masochist at heart; whatever the reason, I moored at the municipal dock for a night. There I met a father and daughter who invited me to join them for dinner aboard their lovely Fisher ketch. They had caught a nice lingcod, and I contributed the bounty from my crab pot. As we dined in their cockpit, a couple stopped by to visit. It was none other than Elsie Hulsizer and her husband, Steve. Elsie is the author of *Voyages to Windward*, a copy of which I had aboard *Pato*.

Voyages to Windward recounts their various voyages up the coast of Vancouver Island the "wrong" way around. Months before, I'd hoped to go up the outside, only to have my plans thwarted by heavy weather at the time.

Also at the dock was a very interesting(!?) boat, preparing to set off on a quest to become the smallest vessel to circumnavigate the globe. She was less than eight feet in length and had a forked spar which carried no mains'l but a single heads'l. It had the appearance of a backyard project created by someone who had smoked a little too much rope; hemp, that is. Perhaps one day that vessel will make its way into written history, hopefully as the smallest vessel to sail around the world and not in a news report about an intrepid adventurer lost at sea.

Thursday, August 24, 1200 hours I cast off the lines and motored out of Tofino via Duffin Pass and Templar Channel. The marine weather forecast was for moderate to strong westerly winds, and I wanted to see how *Pato* would perform beating to weather against the swells.

Unfortunately, the wind was only about five knots, so I decided to troll for a while instead. Almost as soon as my lure hit the water, I had a strike and reeled in a beautiful Chinook salmon. Guess what was going to be on my menu for a few days! After I'd bludgeoned the fish into submission, Slipper gingerly approached my victim. The fish was much larger than she was, but she looked eager to sample a little fresh salmon. I set about filleting my catch on my detachable cleaning table, which I'd secured to the stern rail, and. I had a little more success dismembering this fish, partly due to its being so much larger than my last catch. I was even able to complete the task without dropping him overboard, much to my surprise. Slipper was rewarded with a feast of small morsels I gleaned from the carcass before packaging the rest for future use as crab bait.

With my catch stowed in the refrigerator, I checked the charts for a likely place to anchor for the night. I chose a cove on the east side of Blunden Island. In this location I would be sheltered from the ocean swells, yet the island was small enough that I could hike to the western shore and watch the surf crash on the beach. I skirted Ahous Point and Vargas Island before making my way into the cove, where I anchored at 1600 hours.

I prepared a lovely meal of fresh salmon with new potatoes and dined in the cockpit. From my vantage point I could see the sandy beach of Ahous Bay on Vargas Island's western shore. It felt good to be away from all the activity of Tofino and be back in the wilds, only a few miles distant but worlds apart.

The next morning I rose to a thick fog. As I waited for the sky to clear, I worked on wrapping the wheel. The hours passed, but the fog only got thicker. Eventually, I decided it made sense to stay put for another day.

Taking a break from my project, I rowed to a nearby beach on Blunden Island and made my way through thick brush to the western shore, where the ocean's surf crashed on rocks. I never seem to grow tired of the surf's mesmerizing sound. After a pleasant respite, I returned to *Pato* and picked up my project where I'd left off. It was really beginning to take shape, and I was proud of my efforts.

The fog grew thicker as the day went on and soon even Blunden Island was obscured from view. Yet just above the masthead I could see the bright blue sky. It produced a rather eerie feeling. Although I'd been pinned down by fog all day, I had made the best of it and really had enjoyed my day.

Saturday, August 26 I awoke to fog. I suspected the fog would thicken as the day went on, so I decided to get under way early. I carefully plotted a course that would carry me past any obstacles along the way, and entered a route on my GPS. This would be a test of both my navigation skills and my faith in *Pato's* instruments.

I weighed anchor and motored slowly through the mist, carefully following my route from waypoint to waypoint. Visibility was only about an eighth of a mile, but as I travelled north away from the coast, I left the fog bank behind. As visibility improved, the numerous islets and rocks that I'd plotted my course through came into view. I continued to follow the GPS route and could see that even if visibility had not improved, I would have safely cleared all the obstacles.

Soon I was basking in the sunshine. The wind was only about five knots, so I continued under power past Clifford Point and through Bawden Bay. I rounded Bawden Point and made my way into a nice, sheltered cove behind a couple of small islands in Whitepine Cove, where I settled in for the night.

My surroundings were pleasant, and I still had time to kill, so I decided to spend another lay day. I busied myself exploring the shoreline by dinghy, wandering through the woods, and basking in the sun. I also progressed in wrapping the helm as I continued to hone my marlinspike skills.

Monday, August 28 The month was really earning its nickname of "Fogust." Today was no exception, but the fog began to lift a little early and I got under way at 1000 hours. As much as I loathed Tofino, it was in that direction that I headed. It was the only place I'd found where I could get a strong cell phone signal, and I wanted to check messages and see how the kids were doing.

The wind started out light and flukey, but soon built to a gusty twenty-five knots. Where the wind was strong the seas were short, steep, and confused, so I continued on my way under power. I'd needed to charge the batteries anyway.

I was able to make my phone calls as I approached Tofino. All was well at home, and it was great to hear the kids' voices.

I had no need to go ashore in Tofino, so I motored into the lee of an island across the channel from the village, where I dropped the hook. I soon found that my anchorage was a little too exposed for my liking, so I weighed anchor and made my way back up Lemmens Inlet. I found a lovely cove behind Lagoon Island, where I anchored once more at 1330 hours. This looked like a nice place to hunker down for a few days. Daniel's expected arrival was still more than a week away, and I didn't want to see all there was to see in the area before his arrival.

Across the cove from my anchorage were a couple of floating homes, and I rowed over for a closer look. It has long been my dream to live in a floating house like these, but it is not possible to do so in the U.S. Living aboard my boat was the next best thing. It was interesting to see the various solar panels, solar ovens, and dehydrators they employed. Drinking water came from a poly pipe laid to the shore and up a creek, supplemented by catchment cisterns under their gutter downspouts. They grew vegetables and herbs in pots and boxes on deck. The residents were not home, so I didn't have the opportunity to talk to them and hear their thoughts on their lifestyle. Perhaps it was just as well, as I suspect that they value their privacy.

On another occasion, I followed one of the home's water pipe up a creek. The people who had laid the pipe had cleared a nice trail, and I was able to hike some distance inland. The creek was beautiful and its water sweet and cool. I found a few yew trees along the way and was able to gather a couple of their dead branches which I would fashion into walking sticks.

After several days effort, I put the finishing touches on my helm by tying Turk's Head knots on each of the spokes and one larger Turk's Head on the king spoke, to indicate when the helm was centered. I admired the end result of my efforts, feeling great satisfaction. I know that Brandon would have been impressed.

Next I wrapped the grip of my trusty old walking stick., . This time I tied the Moku Hitch, which employs two lines and makes a decorative diamond pattern that provides a good grip. I finished it off with another Turk's Head knot.

Next I began to fashion another walking stick from one of my yew branches. I began by scraping away the rotten white sap wood, revealing the dark red heartwood. The wood grain was so tight that I could not make out the growth rings, even with a magnifying glass; clearly, this branch had taken many years to grow. I felt that I must show respect for it by utilizing the best craftsmanship I could demonstrate. I carved a grip with a diamond pattern and topped it off with an interesting geometric shape of triangles that combined to form a pyramid and pentagons. The end result was a beautifully crafted walking stick which tapered to only about three-quarters of an inch in diameter.

I liked to demonstrate the strength and flexibility of the yew wood by flexing the stick as far as I could. Unfortunately, I performed this stunt once too often and broke the stick I'd worked so hard to adorn. It had taken all of my strength to break it. I still carry the broken pieces as a memento.

The time was finally approaching for my rendezvous with Daniel. With great anticipation, I prepared to leave Clayoquat Sound behind, for now.

Chapter Twenty-Five

Thursday, August 31 I rowed ashore once more to gather oysters near the mouth of the creek before getting under way at 1230 hours. I motored south down Lemmens Inlet, following the narrow unmarked channel that threads through the shoals.

At one point in the channel there is a "Y" junction, and unfortunately I'd strayed into the wrong leg. This was brought to my attention when I saw eel grass on the bottom moments before *Pato* ground to a halt. Aground again! I checked the tide on my GPS and was relieved to find that low tide was less than an hour away. Soon the tide would be on the rise and float me free.

I made good use of the time by brewing a pot of my famous chili. I decided that if questioned about my predicament, I would claim that I'd grounded on purpose so I could prepare dinner without having to hassle with the anchor. Yea, that was it: I'd planned it!

As expected, *Pato* floated free about an hour after she'd grounded. I did a short turn and doubled back to pick up the channel where I'd missed the turn. Soon I was leaving Lemmons Inlet behind.

I passed by Tofino once more on my way to open water. I learned that the town, which relies heavily on the tourist trade, was basically shut down due to the fact that their water reservoir had run dry. The hot, dry weather that I'd been enjoying for so long had brought swarms of tourists to the village. That was the good news. The bad news was that all of the tourists consumed vast quantities of water that was not being replenished by rain. This was a disaster for the local economy, and was occurring just before the busiest weekend of the year, the "Long Weekend," that coincides with the U.S. Labor Day weekend. I felt a little sheepish about having whined over coughing up quarters for the privilege of filling my water tank. Water, the vital element that makes life on this planet possible, is something we in the northwest frequently take for granted. Perhaps the next time I have to don my rain gear I won't feel as put out.

I motored out Duffin Pass and Templar Channel to reach the Pacific. I was greeted with a nice ten knot northwesterly wind, so I made sail and ran free before the wind, wing-n-wing. The wind rose to fifteen, then twenty knots and I jibed and continued on my way flying a broad reach. Sailing was great and I really enjoyed the feel of the long, gentle swells as they nudged *Pato* along. I stood about a half mile off shore, close enough to enjoy the scenery but far enough off to have a margin of safety if anything should go wrong. I passed Long Beach, then Quisitis Point. I skirted by Florensia Bay close enough to see the waves crash on the rocks and islets at its mouth.

As I followed the shore of the Ucluth Peninsula, the wind began to grow light. I handed the sails and motored into the well-marked north entrance of Ucluelet Inlet. The entrance leads you on the inside of a mass of kelp, which made me think I was following another dead end. Fortunately, my fears were unfounded, and clearing the last light, I turned into the inlet. The last light was in an odd position, which required that you stand well clear lest it lead you onto the rocks.

As I motored up the length of the inlet, I entered familiar waters for the first time in many months. Just two years prior, Daniel and I had traversed this inlet on our first journey onto the waters of the Pacific. I could now say I'd been all the way around Vancouver Island, although not on this trip. (I would refrain from saying I'd circumnavigated Vancouver Island until my inbound track crossed my outbound track from many months ago, an event coming in the not too distant future.) I ducked into the first cove inside the entrance, where I tossed out the hook at 2000 hours and called it a day.

In the morning I weighed anchor and made my way up the inlet to the village of Ucluelet. I stopped at the government dock, which also serves as a customs dock, to top off my water tank. Apparently, Ucluelet did not share Tofino's water woes.

Ucluelet is the port of entry for mariners going up the outside of Vancouver Island, and it is where Daniel and I had cleared customs on our previous visit. We had done so by the phone provided at the dock. The experience provided a stark contrast to the post 911 practices exhibited at U.S. ports of entry. U.S. border agents seem to suspect terrorists are hidden in every nook, cranny, and body cavity; and experience has shown that their defensiveness is not without cause.

With *Pato*'s water tank full, I cast off the lines, putted down the inlet and anchored near the municipal marina. From my anchorage, it was a short row to the dock and the heart of downtown Ucluelet. I would spend a few days hanging around the village. I liked the feel of "Ukee," as many of the locals call it; unlike Tofino, it is not overrun with hordes of tourists. I enjoyed walking the docks, looking at boats and swapping lies with other mariners.

As I rowed back and forth, a few California sea lions would frolic quite close to my dinghy; a little too close for comfort. I grew concerned that they might capsize me. They were usually loitering around the dock awaiting remnants from fishermen's hauls. I heard that someone had recently gotten his fingers bitten when hand-feeding one of the critters; a reminder that it's important to treat wild creatures with respect and caution, no matter how friendly they appear.

I did my laundry, replenished my supplies, and satisfied my cheeseburger craving. I went for long walks along the streets and explored the area parks. Throughout my voyage, the terrain had often been too rugged for a proper hike and my exercise limited to weighing anchor. Ukee was a good place to get a proper cardio workout. Across the peninsula from downtown Ucluelet is a park with a trail that follows the rocky Pacific coast. Along that trail were several places where a recent storm had washed debris high up onto the shoreline, to a height I would not have thought possible. I was once again impressed with the power of nature.

Sunday, September 3 I still had a few days before Daniel's arrival, but had absorbed enough civilization. I weighed anchor at 1200 hours to see a little of Barkley Sound, where I'd once spent a couple of days with Daniel but where much remained to be seen. Conscious of Tofino's water shortage, I stopped once more at Ucluelet's customs dock to top off my water tank before I motored out of the inlet.

Once outside the inlet, I turned *Pato* northeast up Newcombe Channel. When the wind reached ten knots I made sail and continued on a broad reach, enjoying the spectacle of a humpback exuberantly fluking and breaching. A fog bank blew in on twenty knots of wind but left as quickly as it came, and the wind settled in at twelve to fifteen knots. I explored the sound, indulging myself in the joy of sailing amidst magnificent scenery. I passed St Ines Island to port and continued up David Channel to Mayne Bay, where I rounded up and doubled back to the Broken Group's northern outskirts.

I sailed from island to island and cove to cove looking for a quiet anchorage for the night. It seemed every likely spot was already taken by a stink pot (motor boat). I'd forgotten that this was Labor Day weekend, and many yachties were out for their last excursion of the season. I finally found a tiny cove protected by a reef, on Reeks Island. It was just large enough for me to let out adequate scope and not swing onto the reef or shore, and it had the tranquility and privacy I desired. I set the hook at 1900 hours and settled in for the night.

There was a lovely little beach where someone had carefully balanced a number of rocks into a precarious stack. I'd seen similar cairns at Hot Springs Cove and elsewhere, shrines to their builders' wilderness experience. I can only imagine the patience it must take to stack them in this manner. I could scarcely imagine being able to stack two rocks such as these much less several. Later, in the still of the night, I heard a crash on shore. When I rose in the morning I saw that the stack had been toppled by the rising tide. Like the sand paintings of Tibetan Buddhists and some Native American tribes, these shrines were not meant to be permanent.

Joining me in this tiny cove was a vast school of herring, or a "bait ball" which circled *Pato* from the moment I arrived. After darkness fell, I could follow their movement via the phosphorescence that painted glowing trails in their wake. The next morning, as I nursed a pot of coffee and read in my cozy bunk, I heard a noise that could only be a whale's blow. I stuck my head out the hatch just in time to see a humpback blow about fifty feet away, headed in my direction! I scampered on deck, expecting to see him pass directly under *Pato*. Instead, he circled and scooped a huge mouthful of herring before disappearing into the fog. It took a few moments for my heartbeat to settle down from the adrenaline rush.

I waited all day for the fog to lift, but waited in vain. I could see clear blue sky just overhead, but the visibility at sea level was naught. I busied myself working on my walking sticks and enjoying my surroundings, at least what I could see of them.

Tuesday, September 5 I rose again to foggy skies, but eventually the sun burned through and visibility improved. At 1330 hours, I weighed anchor and made my way past the reef and out of the cove. I followed a random, meandering course through the various islands and passages of the Broken Group before wandering into Effingham Bay, where I anchored at 1615 hours.

Daniel and I had visited Effingham Island, the largest island in the Broken Group, on our previous journey. The chart shows a lake on the island, and we had searched for it in vain. This time I resolved to find the lake. I set out on my quest Wednesday morning, armed with a compass and my handheld GPS. I would not be denied! Or would I? I tromped through the woods and up steep hills for hours, and never did find anything resembling a lake. I swear it doesn't exist! I may not have had the swim I'd hoped for, but at least I'd had a good hike and found a lovely beach on the other side of the island. I whiled away the afternoon there, before returning to *Pato* just before sundown.

Thursday, September 7 I rowed over to the adjacent island, where Daniel and I had visited what has to be one of the world's best outhouses. The building is constructed of rough-cut cedar and adorned with all manner of flotsam and jetsam gleaned from the beaches. There is a bucket of sawdust with a large clamshell scoop and a sign instructing you to add one scoop per poop to aid composting. There is a solar powered fan that provides fresh air to the aerobic microbes that convert our waste to useful soil. As I made my contribution to the cause, I contemplated the technology of sewage disposal. Given the all-too-real water crisis Tofino was experiencing and the proven effectiveness of this composting toilet, one has to wonder why we mix several gallons of precious water with our excrement and put it in the ground from which we get our drinking water.

After having had a bowel movement that bordered on a spiritual experience, I returned to *Pato* and prepared to get under way. At 1130 hours I weighed anchor and motored out of Effingham Bay. I turned east and followed Coaster Channel out of the Broken Group. I crossed Imperial Eagle Channel then cut through the Deer Group, yet another beautiful archipelago. Next I crossed Trevor Channel before entering Bamfield Inlet. I tossed out the hook at 1400 hours, in a spot that allowed easy access to both East and West Bamfield.

Bamfield is a small, scenic village, divided by the inlet. It is near the terminus of the West Coast Trail, originally built as a telegraph line and later used as a rescue trail for shipwreck survivors to hike their way back to Victoria. Before modern aids to navigation, Vancouver Island's rugged coast became known as one of the Pacific's graveyards, so numerous were the shipwrecks. Many shipwrecked people made it to shore only to perish from starvation or exposure. The trail gave them at least a fighting chance to live out their days. Today the trail provides a challenging hike through old-growth forest and beaches. It crosses rivers and gorges by suspension bridges and trolleys and is known to be one of the most challenging trails in Canada.

The western part of Bamfield has a beautiful boardwalk that follows the shore for a distance. I rowed ashore and strolled the length of the walk, passing small resorts, bed-n-breakfasts, and small galleries. One gallery's walk is covered with thousands of pennies. Although the shop was not open at the time, I tossed down a few of my own. Farther down the walk I visited another art gallery in an old net shed. I stopped in to check out local artists' wares. Some of the art was quite distinctive. I continued along the boardwalk and arrived at another outhouse of the type found in the Broken Group, which I put to good use. Next I passed a tiny little house of the type that I fantasize building someday. It is a two-story bungalow that occupies a space of about two-hundred square feet; a graphic demonstration that thousands of square feet aren't necessary to create a comfortable home. In this tiny package, they appeared to have a proper kitchen, bath, bedroom, and living room. What more could you need? Eventually the boardwalk ends at the Coast Guard station and dock.

Next, I rowed over to East Bamfield. This side of town has a little more commercial enterprise. There were a couple restaurants and bars, and I took advantage of the opportunity to eat someone else's cooking. East Bamfield is a little more spread out than West Bamfield, and I didn't venture too far from the dock. On my next visit, I'll try to see more of the village.

Daniel called from Neah Bay to let me know that he was on his way and planned to clear customs at Ucluelet the next day. I was somewhat chagrined to learn that Lori had stowed away. Over the years, Daniel and I had learned that more often than not the "two's company, three's a crowd" adage holds true. Daniel assured me that if Lori got in the way of our fun, he would throw her overboard. In any case, we would make the best of it. It had been many months since I'd seen a familiar face, and I eagerly anticipated seeing my dear old friend.

Chapter Twenty-Six

Friday, September 8 The day had finally arrived when I would again see my dear old friend, Daniel. He and I had met about twenty-five years before, when we were both racing motorcycles. Our various adventures on motorcycles produced some of my fondest memories. We had also shared an insatiable appetite for alcohol, then for sobriety, but most important now was our mutual love of sailing.

When I'd spoken to Daniel the day before, we'd acknowledged that we would be out of phone range and have to rely on our VHF radios to establish contact. He had planned on catching the ebb tide out of the Strait of Juan de Fuca and up the coast. We'd estimated an ETA off Bamfield and agreed to contact each other on our radios, select a rendezvous waypoint, enter the waypoint on our GPSs, and set ourselves on a collision course.

At 1100 hours I left Bamfield and proceeded out to the Pacific to do a little trolling, in the hope of providing a feast for my friends. I didn't even get as much as a nibble. Eventually, I raised Daniel on channel sixteen (the hailing channel), and switched to a working channel (sixty-nine, my favorite number) for our conversation. It turned out that he had made much better time than we'd anticipated and was some five miles ahead of me on his way to Ucluelet. I reeled in and set out in pursuit. Visibility deteriorated as I approached Ukee, but I had no problem finding my way to the customs dock.

Vientos de Cambio was already moored at the dock when I arrived, and Daniel and Lori sprung from the companionway to greet me as I pulled in and made *Pato* fast. We exchanged hugs and immediately began debriefing each other on events of the past several months. We went out on the town to share a meal at one of the local eateries, then returned to the dock to spend the night, as moorage was free. We all turned in early, as they had been underway at O-dark thirty in order to catch the tide. Besides, I was exhausted from days of rest and relaxation.

In the morning, we set out on foot to explore Ukee. Lori had never been there, and Daniel had been there briefly, once before. I served as tour guide, having become familiar with the village. We had a great time and before we knew it, we had used up the day. We opted to spend another night at the dock.

Sunday, September 10 we rose to a light fog. As the haze began to lift, we cast off our lines and set out for Hot Springs Cove. When I'd told Daniel about the springs, his mind was made up: he had to see them.

We motored out of Ucluelet Inlet then turned our bows northwest. The wind was about five knots southeasterly but soon rose to about ten knots apparent wind, and we made sail. If *Vientos de Cambio* is a greyhound, *Pato Feo* must be more of a basset hound. I watched *Vientos* forge ahead for a while before reluctantly firing up the engine and motor-sailing in order to keep up. It was just as well, because with our late start we didn't reach Hot Springs Cove until sunset. We handed the sails and motored into the cove, and at 2000 hours I set the hook in a notch in the shore south of the government dock. Daniel brought *Vientos* alongside and rafted up to *Pato*.

As soon as we were sure that we were securely anchored, we rowed over to the dock and set out for the springs. By the time we got there it was completely dark and the sky was splashed with twinkling stars. We stripped and lowered ourselves into a pool. My friends were not disappointed. Daniel and Lori had both been to a number of hot springs before, but both thought that this was the best they had ever encountered.

Monday, September 11 we rose to a bright, beautiful morning. From where we lay, peacefully at anchor in this beautiful, wilderness cove, it was hard to believe that just five years before we had risen to the shocking news of the terrorist attacks that had brought down the twin towers of New York's World Trade Center. How different our world seemed then.

I prepared us one of my famous bachelor scrambles for breakfast, and then we all piled in my dinghy to row across the cove. We rode the last of the ebb through a narrow channel by Mats Island to reach the Pacific shoreline, and climbed around on the rocks, looking for the best vantage point to watch the surf crash on the shore. After a while we'd had enough of playing mountain goat, we rode the flood back through the channel to the cove.

Next, we crossed to the dock and headed to the springs for another soak. My friends were as impressed as I'd been with the craftsmanship of the boardwalk, when they first saw it in daylight. They too admired the names carved on the planks, and praised my handiwork where I'd added *Pato*'s name to the others. We reached the springs in time to watch the sun set over the Pacific. One can scarcely imagine a more idyllic setting. We stayed and soaked until well after full darkness had fallen, and had a nice chat with a young couple from New York who were staying in a lodge at the native village across the cove. It felt completely natural to stand naked with friends and strangers alike in this setting. We soaked until we couldn't stand it anymore, and then we headed back to the boats to call it a night. We were enjoying ourselves so much that we decided to spend another day at the hot springs before we continued on our way.

Wednesday, September 13 we were awakened by the biggest wake you can imagine! One of Daniel's fenders was nearly torn from the lifelines. *Vientos'* toe rail, normally a foot lower than *Pato*'s, had leapt high above my deck and scraped its way down *Pato*'s topsides. My forward starboard portlight had shattered. Fortunately, I'd replaced the portlights' plexiglass with laminated safety glass, so even though the glass shattered, the plastic between the layers of glass had remained intact. This would be important on my return trip should I encounter heavy weather. When *Pato* heels hard over in high winds, the portlights can sometimes be partially submerged. The thin layer of plastic would be relied upon to keep water from entering the cabin. I would have to be cautious about sailing in heavy air until I was able to replace the glass.

It seems that in Canada, no-wake zones are generally ignored. Some boaters seem to have the attitude that if your boat is damaged by their wake, you must not have had your boat properly moored. Regardless, when cruising in Canada, be sure to have lots of fenders, heavy mooring lines, and second thoughts about rafting!

After we'd gotten over our rude awakening and gotten good and coffeed up, we cast off Daniel's lines, and I weighed anchor at 1130 hours, as we set out to continue our adventure. We motored out of

Hot Springs Cove and over to and through Hootla Kootla, then Riley Cove. The wind came up and when it reached ten knots, we made sail. It was nice to sail along and see the familiar and distinctive form of *Vientos de Cambio* as we enjoyed the magic of sailing. Together with *Vientos*, the snow capped mountains of Vancouver Island in the background and the deep blue water flecked with white in the foreground painted a beautiful picture in my memory. We sailed up Sydney Inlet until we reached Adventure Point, where we turned into Holmes Inlet. The first day of autumn was fast approaching, and I knew that the warm, sunny days would soon end, so I opted to take advantage of the weather and sail naked. Alongside my friends, I saw no reason to be embarrassed.

Over our VHF radios we discussed where we would spend the night and decided on Bottleneck Cove. Daniel and Lori forged ahead looking for the cove, but they missed the nearly invisible entrance, which I found and proceeded through under sail. Once in the bottleneck, the wind was light, but I was able to maintain three knots into the cove. Once inside, the cove opened up and I was able to sail around looking for the best place to anchor. When I'd found a satisfactory spot, I dropped the anchor and handed the sails. I tried to raise Daniel on the radio, but the signal was blocked by the rocky hills surrounding the cove. As he'd been searching for the cove, he'd been watching me bring up the rear. One moment I was there; the next I was gone! He sailed back and forth for a while before he finally found the entrance, and he too sailed through. It was obvious to us all where the name Bottleneck Cove came from!

We rafted up again, but this time we were confident that no wake would disturb us, as there were no signs of civilization in the cove. We shared another meal and kicked back to drink in the beauty that surrounded us. We sat out in our cockpits talking well into the night. Eventually we stumbled down our companionways to our warm bunks; Daniel had Lori to warm his bunk, and I had Slipper to warm mine. Somehow it didn't seem quite the same. Sorry, Slipper!

Thursday, September 14 we got underway at 1100 hours. It was calm in the cove, but just outside the entrance, we could see that the wind was blowing. As we motored out we were greeted with fifteen knots, enough to move *Pato* along at a good clip, but not enough to overpower *Vientos*. We couldn't ask for better conditions! We made sail and beat to weather, making our way back through Holmes and Sydney Inlets. We sailed into Steamer Cove and ghosted past George Island, which blocked our wind, then continued on our way along Shelter Inlet to Obstruction Island.

When I'd passed this way before, I'd gone through Hayden Passage, so this time we decided to go around the other side of Obstruction Island via Sulphur Passage, despite the chart's notation, "local knowledge required." Daniel has a bit of an adventurous spirit and seems to fear nothing. His willingness or eagerness to throw caution to the wind has not yet led to our demise, despite his best efforts. Sometimes I think he is a bad influence on me. This time however, it was the other way around; I led the way into the narrow, rock-strewn, zigzag passage under a full press of canvas!

As we entered the passage, we had to turn nearly 180° around a reef that would have been unseen were it not for the kelp that indicated its position. Sometimes kelp is our friend! In the passage, winds were flukey as hell, blowing from all points of the compass and at speeds anywhere from zero to twenty knots. As we beat our way through, I led the way. I would sail as close as I dared to the steep, rocky shore before tacking, thankful for my self-tending jib, which greatly simplified the task of tacking in these narrow confines. Daniel had his hands full, as *Vientos* was overpowered in the frequent puffs. As he tacked back and forth, he would put the helm hard a'lee and backwind the genoa to bring the bow through the wind before cutting loose the weather sheet and trimming for the new tack. At one point in the passage, we encountered a fishing boat that further restricted the narrow channel. Since he was engaged in fishing, he had the right of way, and I thought we did an admirable job of staying clear of him. He obviously had the "local knowledge" that we lacked and probably shook his head at the crazy Yanks who were venturing through the passage under sail. After one more sharp turn, we encountered the narrowest part of the passage and were exposed to the full force of the wind.

As we emerged from Sulphur Passage and entered Miller Channel, we were greeted by a rain squall carried in on heavy wind. The rain was short lived, and the wind dropped to a more manageable level as we sailed into Matilda Inlet. We continued past the village of Ahousat to the end of the inlet, where we rafted at anchor at 1900 hours, just in time to enjoy the sunset. It had been a memorable and exciting day, and we were all exhausted, so we turned in early.

The next day we decided to take a lay-day. As we were nursing our coffee in the cockpit, I saw something in the water crossing the channel. I pointed it out to Daniel and he quickly grabbed his binoculars. To our surprise, it was a black bear! When he travels, Daniel is always on the lookout for bears and more often than not, none are to be found. Who would have thought that when he finally found one it would be in the water?!

After breakfast, I clambered aboard *Vientos* and we cast off the lines, leaving *Pato* at anchor. We motored over to the native village of Marktosis, which lies on a narrow isthmus in the peninsula separating Matilda Inlet from Millar Channel. I'd read that the entrance was very rocky and that you would want to use your dinghy, and to be sure to secure everything that you didn't want to come up missing while at the dock. We had no problem finding our way through the rocks to the dock, and *Vientos* was unmolested during our visit. I'd also read that there was a nice, modern market there, but try as we might, we couldn't find it. Eventually, we asked a local where it could be found and were told that no such market existed. We strolled across the isthmus to a nice sandy beach on Millar Channel, where we were approached by a young man in uniform who asked us if we had paid our beach users fee. We were about to get upset, as we could scarcely imagine such a ridiculous thing, when we caught the slightest gleam in his eye. He was only kidding. He had in fact only come over to say hi and ask where we were from. If I were a poker player, I would not want to be sitting across the table from this guy!

When we'd seen what there was to see of Marktosis, we cast off and made our way over to Ahousat on the other side of the inlet. There we found a wonderful general store that looked as if it had been there forever. They had a little of everything, from groceries to fishing tackle to marine hardware and anything else you might imagine. It was like stepping back in time to shop there. There was a "for sale" sign on the building that looked as if it had been there for many years. We bought what we needed and went next door to have lunch at a little café, where we were the only patrons. We were glad to have left a few dollars in the hands of folks trying to eke out a living in this backwater.

Later in the afternoon, we again rafted *Vientos* alongside *Pato* and rowed to the end of the inlet to the aptly named "warm springs." These certainly would not be mistaken for hot springs, as the water was merely tepid. There was a rectangular concrete tub, large enough to hold several people, a far cry from the natural setting and hot water found at Hot Springs Cove. We continued past the tub and followed a trail off into the woods toward the Pacific coast. As we walked, we were sure to make a lot of noise, since we knew bears were in the area. We walked through the forest and a nice meadow before emerging at Whitesand Cove, which had a broad sandy beach. There we spent some time beachcombing and frolicking in the sand. On our way back, we stopped to bathe in the tub before returning to our waiting boats.

Saturday, September 16 Ever have one of those days when it just doesn't pay to get out of bed?

We weighed anchor and set out for Blunden Island, where you may recall that I'd spent a few pleasant days waiting for the fog to clear. We motored north out of Matilda Inlet after pausing at Ahousat for fuel. When we reached the mouth of the inlet, we turned south and followed the shoreline past the beach at Marktosis. By the time we'd reached Yates Point, less than a mile away, I knew it wasn't my day. My compass and GPS told me to veer away from shore, but my mind kept telling me to follow the shoreline. I was completely disoriented and couldn't seem to figure out where I was.

Since I'd spent some time in these waters, Daniel was following me, but he soon realized something was amiss. He hailed me on the radio to ask where the heck I was going, and I replied that I didn't know where the @#$% I was! (And yes, I did break with proper radio etiquette by using profanity over the air; such was my frustration.) I took my way off to find my position on the chart and check my course. I still couldn't convince myself that the instruments were right. It was a rather disconcerting feeling to say the least! I told Daniel of my uneasy feelings, and he was very understanding when

I told him I was going to reverse course and head once again for nearby Quait Bay.

Daniel decided they would join me after they paused at the estuary of the Cypre River in the hope of seeing some more bears. (They were not disappointed.) I proceeded into Quait Bay and anchored to await their arrival and collect my thoughts. What was it that had caused me to forget or ignore everything I'd learned about navigation? I couldn't come up with an explanation, so I just let it go. Given that the course my mind was telling me to follow was heading directly toward a reef, giving up was the prudent thing to do.

A few hours later, *Vientos* pulled in and anchored across the cove from where *Pato* lay. Daniel seemed to sense that I needed to regroup. Later, the weather took a turn for the worse when a heavy rain began to fall. Due to the water shortage being felt at the time, I decided to take full advantage of the heavy rain. I rigged a new poly tarp over the foredeck to catch water in as many empty jugs as I had aboard. I also decided to bathe in the warm rain. I stripped, went out on the foredeck, and lathered up. I realized that it was going to take a while for the rain to rinse off the soap, when I noticed that my dinghy was about half full of water. I scampered over the side and was soon taking a bath in the dinghy. Daniel hailed across the cove to ask what I was doing and I replied, "What's it look like I'm doing? I'm takin' a bath!" They had a good laugh.

The next morning, we rowed ashore and hiked up a creek bed to a lake, where we took a refreshing dip in the cold water. We had a great time and felt all "new and improved" as we headed back for the boats. It was a little too late to be getting underway by the time we got back, so we opted to spend another night.

Monday, September 19 the time had come for Daniel and Lori to start heading for home, as they both needed to get back to work. We decided to get an early start and were underway at 0900 hours. We motored down the now familiar Maurus Channel to one of the islands near Tofino, where I anchored. I wanted to be near the "exit," so this seemed a likely staging area. Daniel chose to forge ahead, intent on fetching Ucluelet. The weather forecast wasn't good, but he decided to see firsthand what the conditions were like and thought if it grew too rough, he could always retreat and seek shelter. A short time later, Daniel hailed me on the radio to tell me it wasn't so bad once you were well clear of shore. Since there was plenty of daylight remaining, I weighed anchor and set out for Ukee after all. Just as Daniel had described, it was really sloppy in Templar Channel, but it smoothed out a little when I reached open water. The wind was southeasterly eighteen knots, which was perfect for *Pato*, but it was rough enough that I didn't want to venture onto the foredeck to make sail. Besides, I was now committed to fetching Ukee and needed to make up miles.

Just before I reached the point where I would be out of cell phone range, my phone rang to indicate that I had a voicemail. When I went to check my mailbox, I was shocked to see that Peewee had left thirty-seven messages! I could see that she had called, but my signal was too weak to actually retrieve the messages, much less call her back. I cannot even begin to describe the anxiety I felt as I slowly made my way toward Ucluelet, where I knew I'd be able to call. Time seemed to stand still, and I bumped up the engine RPM to increase *Pato*'s speed. In the hours that passed, I imagined any number of reasons she would have called so frequently. My greatest fear was that one of the kids had had an accident. Countless times, I tried to call but the signal was too weak to make a connection.

After what seemed an eternity, I turned the corner and headed up Ucluelet Inlet. At last I had a strong signal and began to listen to her messages. All she said was, "Call me, please call me!" She had said the same thing, message after message, but with each successive message her speech became more slurred. Obviously, she was drinking with a vengeance. I wasted little time listening to more, braced myself for the worst, and dialed her phone. She answered immediately. "Is there another woman?" she asked.

I was beyond incredulous; I was enraged! At that instant I went supernova! How could she have put me through the agonizing hours of not knowing, the fear, the anxiety, the outright terror? And for what? For this?! No I was not seeing another woman, and what if I was? We were divorced, remember?! I unleashed a torrent of the most abusive language I could glean from my substantial vocabulary of blue words. If I could have come up with anything worse to say, I would have gladly used it.

Obviously, Iowa had done nothing to help with her addiction to alcohol, and she had picked up right where she had left off. I was even more disturbed to think what this was doing to the kids.

I was in a daze as I pulled alongside the customs dock and made *Pato* fast at 1830 hours. Daniel and Lori had made good time and had continued on to Bamfield in order to be that much closer to home. I was actually glad that they were not there to see me so upset. My mind was in such turmoil that I couldn't even feel the relief of knowing that a disaster had not befallen one of the kids. I had a fitful, restless night and slept little.

Part Four

I've Taken the Time to Live

Chapter Twenty-Seven

Tuesday, September 19 It was another bright, sunny morning, but my head was foggy from lack of sleep. It had been a rough night. The rage of the night before was replaced with a dull ache in my heart. Over the course of my journey, I'd found peace. I'd found a new direction for my life, a new love in my life, the sea. If I were to live out my days alone, I would live them happily.

Peewee on the other hand was on a path of self-destruction, her downward spiral apparently well lubricated with prodigious quantities of alcohol. Her once-promising career was gone, and though I didn't know it at the time, her lovely home would soon follow. She simply could not let go of the past; our past.

I called her and apologized for my tirade of the day before. She offered no apologies for what she had put me through. I finally came to the conclusion that there was nothing I could do to save her from herself.

I could only guess how Jason and Nicole were doing under the circumstances. I knew that I needed to be there for them and, hopefully, help them find the strength to cope. More importantly, I needed to help each of them, in any way I could, follow their unique path, the one they alone could choose. It was time to go home.

In preparation for getting underway, I listened to the weather forecast, which predicted changeable conditions but didn't sound too bad. I bought a few provisions and topped off the water tank. I plotted a course for Port San Juan and entered a route on my GPS before casting off the lines at 1100 hours and proceeding out of port. My route was the most direct possible, but I still knew that it would be full dark when I arrived at my destination. Off Barkley Sound I encountered a little fog but it cleared before I reached Cape Beale. A northwesterly wind came up, and when it reached ten knots I made sail. The wind rose to fifteen knots and I was making good time but soon realized that if I were to fetch Port San Juan at a reasonable hour I would need to motor-sail. I cranked up the engine. Soon the fog was back with a vengeance and visibility was reduced to about an eighth of a mile. I was caught out. The weather forecast had not predicted fog, but here it was, and I was committed. I found myself wishing for radar and an automatic fog signal. I was not in the least concerned with losing my way in the fog (as I'd regained my confidence in my GPS, compass, and my navigational skills), but what did concern me was the possibility of a collision. My route kept me about a mile off shore, well out of the shipping lanes, but I did encounter the occasional fishing boat.

At twilight I handed the sails and continued under power into the night. It was a new moon, so when it got dark, it was really dark, but at least the fog got thicker! When I turned on my navigation lights, my portside light chose to blink out, and I was forced to use my masthead tri-color light together with my steaming light. Since your steaming light is supposed to be above and abaft your side lights, not below them, this combination may have been a little confusing to other mariners; that is if they could see me at all.

It was a rather eerie feeling being in a fog so thick it threatened to obscure my own bow. In the diffused light of my steaming light, I could see the odd strands of spider webs as they gathered on the shrouds. I caught a glimpse of something up by the masthead light. It was there and then it was gone. Was I imagining things? There it was again! Now my attention was fully focused on trying to figure out what it was that I saw. It returned again, and this time I was able to make out what it was that had gotten my attention. It was a couple of hummingbirds! What were they doing out here, so far from shore in the middle of the night?! Then it occurred to me that they were probably migrating south for the winter and had lost their way in the fog and darkness. They seemed to take comfort in my light, and they followed me on my way. I told them, "Don't follow me, I'm lost too!" but they took no heed. They were still with me as I approached my destination of Port San Juan.

Port San Juan offers little in the way of protected anchorages, but when Daniel and I had been this way before, we had found shelter behind Woods Nose, a rock outcrop on the southeast shore of the port. There we had found enough room for one boat to anchor comfortably. Fortunately, I had my log book of that voyage with me and I had recorded the exact position in which we had anchored.

This proved to be very useful information indeed. My GPS route kept me well clear of Owen Point and led me to the lighted buoy off the mouth of Port San Juan, then to a point just off Woods Nose, and finally to the waypoint I'd entered from my old log. Following my route, I could make out the loom of the light before it hove into view just as expected. I continued on to my next waypoint, where I turned directly toward the unseen shore. My GPS counted down the feet once I was less than a tenth of a mile from my waypoint. As I approached my destination, I watched the numbers tick downward. When my GPS indicated that I was within fifty feet of my waypoint, I could begin to make out the lights of a home on shore. As I covered the last fifty feet, my depth sounder also counted down, and when my GPS sounded the alarm to announce my arrival at my destination I was in thirty feet of water. Ain't technology grand?! I dropped the hook at 2230 hours and immediately threw myself into the bunk. I was relieved to be through with navigating in the fog.

Wednesday, September 20 I got underway early and headed east along the Strait of Juan de Fuca, planning on stopping at Sooke Harbor for the night. Daniel and I had stopped there on our last journey and had enjoyed the atmosphere at the dock. Winds were light and variable and although the sky was overcast, visibility was good, much to my relief. I had no desire to endure another passage in the fog.

I was making good time and decided to proceed on to Becher Bay. I'd never been there before, and one of the purposes of my journey was to see new places. Approaching Becher Bay I rounded Beechey Head and saw an inviting park on the shore. I nestled in close to shore and dropped the hook. I waited awhile to make sure the anchor was holding; although this was a weather shore, it was a little exposed for my liking. When I was satisfied that *Pato* was secure, I splashed the dink and rowed ashore for a walk.

The park had once been a large farm, and there remained beautiful pastures and orchards as well as nice beaches and woods. I had a great walk; it felt good to stretch my legs. I walked to the other side of a point where I saw that there was a more secure anchorage and decided to move *Pato* there. I settled in for what was to be my last night in Canadian waters.

Thursday, September 21, 1000 hours I weighed anchor, reflecting on the events of the past months. Memories of places, people, wildlife, and experiences came flooding back; memories that will be with me always. I still had some distance to travel to reach home, but I felt as if my journey was over. I found myself in a somewhat subdued mood.

I plotted a course that would carry me across the Strait of Juan de Fuca to Port Angeles, where I would clear customs. The forecast was for thirty knot winds in the strait, so while I was still well inside Becher Bay and somewhat sheltered, I made sail. I opted to venture out under reduced sail however, so I'd hanked on the jib and raised the mizzen, leaving the main stowed on the boom. Out in the strait I encountered great sailing conditions. The wind was northwesterly fifteen knots and the seas were far from unmanageable. I decided *Pato* could carry more canvas, so I raised the main, but with a double reef as I still expected the wind to build. The wind increased to twenty knots and settled, so I shook the reefs out of the main. Allowing for some leeway and current I sailed a broad reach on a heading a little west of my destination. *Pato* felt alive beneath me and I felt at one with her. These were the ideal conditions for *Pato* and I reveled in the feeling of being part of the boat, or perhaps her being part of me. We were as one. As I approached the strait's mid-point, I found that our leeway was not as severe as I'd predicted so I fell off and ran free before the wind, flying wing-n-wing.

I felt a degree of sadness as I left Canada behind. The trees of Vancouver Island grew smaller and indistinct before blending into a mass; the mountains dropped further and further into the background. I watched the lighthouse at Race Rocks fade from view, and then turned my attention ahead as the Washington coast grew near and the Olympic Mountains spread across the horizon. Soon the lighthouse at Ediz Hook hove into view. As I jibed and rounded the hook, the feeling of sadness faded away and was replaced with an eagerness to see familiar faces, especially Jason's and Nicole's.

In the lee of the hook, I handed the sails and proceeded to the city dock. I called U.S. customs, and they dispatched an officer to meet me at the dock. I pulled alongside and made *Pato* fast. I waited awhile and soon the customs officer arrived. He asked me if I had anything to declare. I reflected for a moment before saying no. What I'd acquired while in Canada were memories. What mementos I had acquired were things I'd found along the way: a feather, a rock, a piece of beach glass, a stick. These things were of no value, but they were priceless.

While I was in Port Angeles, I contacted my friend, Nancy, who lived in the area. She had been going through a divorce about the same time I had, and we'd commiserated from time to time. She was eager to see me and asked if I might like to accompany her to a Cajun dance at Port Townsend the next day. I could stay at the city dock for up to forty-eight hours for free, and I needed to do laundry and some boat maintenance anyway, so why not?

I set out on foot with my bag of laundry and eventually found a laundromat. With my clean laundry, I returned to *Pato*, pausing to treat myself to a bag of pipe tobacco which had been both difficult to find and expensive in Canada. I spent a little time tidying up *Pato*; she was looking a little "lived in," and I didn't want Nancy to see her like that.

The next morning, Nancy picked me up and we drove to Port Townsend. We stopped at a chandlery so I could pick up a few odds and ends, and then headed for the dance at the Grange Hall. They gave us a brief lesson on the traditional dance steps, but their efforts were wasted on me; I was hopeless! When the dancing began, Nancy and I moved around the room as best we could, as we followed the other dancers. I broke away to use the restroom and found a mop propped in the corner. When I returned to the dance floor, I had a new partner and did we show them some moves! She was very slender, had stringy hair and was a little stiff. Everyone had a good laugh at me and my mop. We had a great time. Later, when Nancy dropped me off at *Pato*, I persuaded her to join me for a sail to Sequim the next day.

Saturday, September 23 was the autumnal equinox, the first day of fall. It was also five months to the day since I'd embarked on my voyage. As we'd planned, Nancy joined me at the dock. We cast off the lines and set out for Sequim Bay. We had hoped to have a nice day of sailing, but, Mother Nature was not cooperating; it was flat calm. We had a very pleasant visit as we motored along in the bright sunlight. I prepared us a simple lunch and we shared it in the cockpit. We cruised along the southern shore of the strait until we cleared Dungeness Spit, where we turned toward our destination.

Too soon, we approached the entrance to Sequim Bay which is well marked with buoys. It is important that you heed the markers, lest you run aground. Don't be fooled by appearances or try to follow shallow draft speed boats, which are able to zoom over the shoals with impunity. As you follow the shoreline of the strait, it is tempting to head directly for the opening at the end of the spit. Do so and you will find yourself aground. But wait; there's more! As you clear the spit, the bay opens up before you. Again you will be tempted, this time to head for open water in the middle of the bay. Do so and you will encounter yet another shoal. The entrance is straightforward and well marked, so it is not difficult, but it is necessary to pay attention. We motored into John Wayne Marina, named for the movie star who was an American icon and had kept his yacht, a converted World War Two minesweeper, here. I dropped Nancy at the dock and we said our goodbyes, then she caught a ride back to Port Angeles with a friend.

Nancy was planning to move back to Vashon Island soon, where she had lived for many years and where we had met. Vashon is relatively close to my home in Port Orchard. We agreed to keep in touch and planned to see each other again when she got settled. Nancy and I would indeed get together soon and embark on a brief but beautiful romance. Perhaps she was my "transitional relationship," a term favored by a woman I'd tried to woo who was a psychologist. If I was to have a transitional relationship, I can think of no one I would rather have had it with. Nancy is a sweet, wonderful lady and if I have any regret, it would be for any pain I may have caused her when I broke it off. Unfortunately, I've lost contact with her due to the fact that I simply couldn't face her after the way I'd treated her. We should have become the best of friends. She deserved better. Lesson learned.

After I'd dropped Nancy off, I cast off once more, proceeded a little further into the bay, and anchored. I busied myself performing some long-neglected boat maintenance. I'd not changed the engine oil since I left home, and while at the chandlery, I'd bought a vacuum oil-sucker-outer so I could finally perform this vital task. The stuff I sucked out of the crankcase still looked like oil, but was it black; very black! I convinced myself that it had retained some lubrication qualities; after all, what turned it black was carbon residue from burning fossil fuel, and carbon and graphite are almost the same thing. Graphite is a dry lubricant, so therefore, the carbon in my oil actually aided in lubrication. Yea, that's it! Black oil is better! All of the mechanical engineers in the world who insist that clean oil is good only say so because they are all puppets of the big oil companies. It's clearly a global conspiracy! Beware the maintenance mongers!

Sunday, September 24, 0930 hours I got underway and set out for Port Townsend. When I cleared the entrance of Sequim Bay, I followed Miller Peninsula's shoreline. It was again flat calm and sunny, so I proceeded under power. I passed between Protection Island and Discovery Bay, then along the shore of the Quimper Peninsula to Point Wilson.

When I rounded the buoy off the Point Wilson lighthouse, I had completed my circumnavigation of Vancouver Island. I felt a sense of accomplishment and pride. I turned my attention back the way I'd come and watched as the mountains of Vancouver Island disappeared from view behind the point. Farewell, Canada!

As I approached Point Hudson and prepared to head into Port Townsend, the wind began to build. It soon reached fifteen knots, so I decided to continue under sail. I hanked on the genoa and set sail, running free before the sweet northwesterly breeze, flying wing-n-wing. After a few days of flat calm, it was a welcome breeze indeed. At Marrowstone Point, I jibed and sailed a broad reach along Admiralty Inlet, hugging the shore of Marrowstone Island. I had no particular destination in mind; I would simply sail away the rest of the day and duck into the most convenient anchorage to present itself in these familiar waters. To starboard, I passed by Mats Mats Bay with its narrow entrance channel, where I'd once practiced following range markers. Next I passed Port Ludlow, where I'd once found shelter from a blow behind the Twin Islands at the head of the bay. I crossed the mouth of Hood Canal. Daniel and I had visited Port Gamble, a short distance down the canal, aboard *Pamplonica*. I passed Fowlweather Bluff, then Point No Point. As I left Admiralty Inlet and proceeded into Puget Sound, to port I passed the mouth of Possession Sound where I'd once sat out a heavy fog in the Port of Everett. Next to starboard came Apple Cove Point, where I'd once been surrounded by a pod of orcas. As I rounded the point, Mount Rainier hove into view. I'd been born in the shadow of the mountain. I could see Seattle's skyline in the distance and knew I was nearly home. As the sun set over Appletree Cove, I tossed out the hook across from the town of Kingston at 1900 hours. This was the first place I'd ever sailed onto the hook, which I'd had to do when *Laughing Wind's* engine had failed to start. Daniel and I had noted that all journeys seem to begin and end in Kingston. Perhaps there is something akin to the pull of gravity that seems to draw us there. More likely, it is just in a convenient location, but who knows?

It had been yet another wonderful day. I sat in the cockpit until well after dark, not wanting the day to end.

Monday, September 25 I rose early and prepared to get underway. At 0900 hours, I made sail, then weighed anchor and sailed off the hook as I continued to practice anchoring and getting underway without the engine. Mariners had done so for thousands of years, so why couldn't I? Besides, that way I'll be better prepared for the day when we've used the last drop of petroleum.

The wind was light and variable in the cove and I soon found myself in irons, so I had to start the engine just long enough to get some way on and fall off. Outside the cove, the wind was northwesterly about ten knots, and I set out on a broad reach down the sound. I sailed past President Point, where I'd once hooked a beautiful silver salmon, only to have my line break just as I got him to the boat; a classic case of "the one that got away." Next I came to Port Madison, where I've spent many a night at anchor, and the entrance to Agate Pass, which I had traversed as I departed on my voyage months ago.

I considered stopping at Eagle Harbor a little farther down the east side of Bainbridge Island. This was once a haven for a thriving community of aquatic vagabonds who lived on a ramshackle fleet of dilapidated boats scattered about the harbor. Their numbers are gradually diminishing under mounting pressure from the homeowners around the harbor, who don't want their views blighted by what they see as vagrancy. Eagle Harbor has long been a favorite destination of mine. On this day, however, the wind seemed to have other plans for me, and I found myself off Shilshole Bay. You may recall that Shilshole Bay Marina was where I'd met Joe, from whom I'd bought *Pato Feo*. That coincidental meeting of two people from different walks of life had made this entire journey possible.

The wind shifted off West Point, and soon *Pato* was drawn toward Blake Island, another of my familiar haunts. Blake Island is a state park accessible only by water. There you will find Tillicum Village, a Native American-themed restaurant and cultural center that serves salmon dinners prepared in the traditional ways. While you dine, they perform native dances for your entertainment. It is a far cry from the genuine cultural experience I had found in far away Alert Bay.

I was now only a few short miles from home, and I decided to call Kelly and Linda of Blues Power, whom I'd met in my travels and who lived aboard at nearby Brownsville Marina. They had returned from their voyage awhile back, but had decided to take off on their boat for a couple of days. As luck would have it, they were currently moored at, you guessed it, Blake Island! While I was talking to Kelly, Otto (my autopilot) had the helm. I did not change course by even as much as one degree, and soon I found myself sailing directly into the anchorage east of Blake Island. Apparently this is just where I was supposed to be. I rounded up and dropped the hook before handing the sails. I splashed the dink and rowed ashore to visit with Kelly and Linda for a while, before returning to *Pato*.

I sat out on deck as daylight faded into night. In the dying light, snowcapped Mount Rainier turned from stark white to pink, then purple, before disappearing into the blackness of night. Across the sound, the lights of Seattle twinkled gold in the near distance. The first star appeared, then another and another, then more still. Soon they filled the night sky with their light.

I heard sounds that had become so familiar over the past months that I would usually take no notice. The gurgle of the water as the current flowed round *Pato*'s hull, and the ripples as they slapped against her; the softest whisper of a breeze through the rigging. On this night, I noticed. These were the sounds that meant all was well.

I called Daniel to let him know my whereabouts. He described how he'd felt at the end of his Alaska adventure; he described what I was feeling at that very moment. I smoked one more pipe and went below to my bunk. Slipper laid on my legs, as she nearly always does, expressing her contentment by purring loudly. I slept.

Tuesday, September 26 I awoke at 0700 hours. I consumed a pot of coffee in my bunk, then another as I read my latest book. Through my open hatch, I heard the drone of an approaching small plane and spotted a flash of red. I clambered out on deck as Daniel banked steeply into a turn and passed again at masthead height before wiggling his wings in greeting and heading southeast. He'd flown out in his Cessna to welcome me home.

I was no more than an hour from my home in Port Orchard, but I was not in a particular rush to get there. At 0900 hours I made sail and weighed anchor, but instead of heading for home, I headed in the opposite direction, toward Alki Point and West Seattle. The northwesterly wind was about twelve knots and I just felt like sailing. I didn't want my trip to end. I came to realize, however, that there was no point in further delaying the inevitable, so I tacked and turned *Pato*'s bow toward home.

As I entered Rich Passage and fell into the lee of Bainbridge Island, the wind went flat, as it nearly always does. I started the engine and motor-sailed through. I had hoped to arrive home under sail, as I'd left, but as I emerged from the passage and entered Port Orchard, I could see that it was flat calm all the way across to the end of Sinclair Inlet. I gave the controls to Otto as I handed the sails and put on the covers. I scooped up buckets of water and sluiced the deck; I wanted *Pato* to look shipshape, although no one would ever call her Bristol fashion.

To starboard, I passed Port Washington Narrows with its aging Manette Bridge framing the Olympic Mountains, then Bremerton and the Puget Sound Naval Shipyard. I saw the imposing silhouette of the "Hammerhead" crane, which was once able to lift entire sixteen inch gun turrets out of battleships. The ferry *Kitsap* pulled away from the dock and set out for Seattle. The old *Carlyle II* pulled in from Port Orchard across the inlet. And there off my port bow was the town of Port Orchard that I'd come to call home. I made my last turns into the fairway and slotted into my empty slip. As I made *Pato* fast, the clock tower struck twelve and its bells pealed their tune. I was home.

Epilogue

No fanfare or marching bands greeted me when I returned home to Port Orchard. There was no ticker tape parade, no hero's welcome. Walking downtown I encountered faces I'd come to know. "Hiya, haven't seen ya in a while, where ya been? Whatcha been up to?"

I retrieved Gertrude from where I'd left her and set out to see my friends: Daniel and Lori, Ed and Mary Jo, Jim and Charlotte, Mom and Pop (Daniel's, that is, I've made them my own), all the usual suspects. I took Jason and Nicole out to dinner. We hugged, we cried.

Over the next few months, I took several short journeys around my home waters of the Puget Sound. Spending five months at sea had only whetted my appetite for more.

What did I learn in my travels? I learned the power of dreams. We all have them, but for many, they remain only that; dreams.

When we were young, we were asked, "What do you want to be when you grow up?" and we replied, _____ (insert your dream), based on our TV heroes on or those we learned about in school.

As we grew a little older, our dreams may have changed a little; I no longer wanted to be the president of the United States, I wanted to be a world champion motorcycle racer. Still later in life, I dreamed of being a ferry captain.

These are the dreams of how we will sustain ourselves, how we will earn a living. Many measure their success in life by the prestige and accolades bestowed upon those in their profession; others by how much money they earn. And there are those of us who feel that success cannot be measured in dollars and cents. Live your dreams, but never confuse what you do with who you are.

Some may dream of conquering the financial world, of buying the biggest mansion, the biggest yacht, and the fanciest cars. There are many who measure their success in life by the things they own. If that is your dream, pursue it!

Others may dream of a simpler life, of living on a self-sustaining farm and raising their own food; or living in a hut in the woods and living off the land; or living in a little boat and gleaning their sustenance from the bounty of the sea. Find your dream and live it!

We dream of the things we hope to achieve in life. We may hope to save humanity, or save the earth, or save souls; all lofty goals. Each of us can play a part in achieving these ends. Perhaps you will find the cure for cancer. Perhaps you will save the whales. Perhaps you will find a way that people of all religions can coexist and end the conflict and bloodshed in the name of God. It's a big universe we live in and there's room for lots of 'em.

And then there are the dreams that have nothing to do with how we earn a living. Some may dream of learning to fly; others of climbing Mount Rainier, or hiking the length of the Appalachian Trail, or traveling Europe in an old VW bus, or riding a motorcycle the length of the Americas. If you've read this book, you probably have dreamt of cruising the San Juan Islands or the inside passage to Alaska, or around the world. You may have even bought a boat that sits in a marina waiting for "someday," while you sit in your office longing for that day. Cast off the lines and get underway! Don't let yourself utter with your dying breath, "I wish I would have"!

When I embarked on this adventure, I set out to fulfill a dream. With that dream fulfilled, the question arose, "What's next?" Not long after I returned to port, I enrolled in a class at Port Hadlock where I passed the examinations for my U.S. Coast Guard 100 ton Masters license, which I obtained the week after my fifty-second birthday. I went on to become a relief skipper on the *Charlie Wells* in hope of someday being part of the permanent crew: thereby fulfilling another dream.

And what of matters of the heart? Now there is a complex question! I learned that one cannot make another whole; that we must be whole in and of ourselves before we can ever hope to become part of a greater whole as a couple. Don't count on your mate to complete you.

In any successful relationship, there is give and take. Like the ebb and flow of the tide, sometimes we give, sometimes we receive.

However, if we compromise ourselves, our principals, our dreams for another, we will eventually be reduced to nothingness and have no more to give. Do not ask more of another than you are willing to give, nor give more than you hope to receive. A stream not replenished by rain will eventually run dry.

Don't settle for an unfulfilling relationship out of fear of being alone. Be happy in your own skin. If you look like you're having fun in your sandbox, others will want to play too!

Which brings us full circle, to a brief moment that is forever etched in my memory. Less than a year later, I was working as skipper on the *Charlie Wells*. We were at the mainland dock, preparing to get underway for Herron Island. I'd strolled up to the head of the dock to see what kind of load we had. There on that familiar shore, within sight of the island I loved, with *Pato* lying peacefully at anchor off its shore, I caught a glimpse of a beautiful woman sitting on a log with Donnie's wife, Suzie. I was tempted to go over and say hi, but I sensed sadness and let them be. Instead, I asked Donnie who was with Suzie. In his fading Texas drawl, he replied simply, "That's Lorrruh." Meet Lara.

> *Once upon a sun bleached shore*
> *I gazed upon a maiden fair*
> *Gently was the salty breeze*
> *Wafting through her flaxen hair …*

Laugh, cry, love, hope, dream, live!

Take the time to live!

Fin

Postscript

Lara and I were to become involved in a sometimes-beautiful and sometimes-tumultuous three year relationship, which has now ended. If I am never again to find love, I will always be grateful for having at least once in my life experienced that kind of passion. She was my muse.

My new career as a captain has exceeded my wildest fantasies. Two years after obtaining my master's license, I was hired by a small company that conducts dining cruises in Seattle. I operate a variety of vessels, ranging from 64 feet to 105 feet, and I meet thousands of people from all walks of life. For someone who pontificates that one should not confuse their profession with their identity, it is ironic that friends and acquaintances call me Captain. Astute readers will note the contradiction.

I've now taken to living ashore, but the waters of Puget Sound are no more than a glance away outside my windows. The water is my life, and life is good!

apparent wind: the combination of the true wind and that caused by your own motion

aft: toward the stern or rear, behind

backing down: engaging reverse gear to set the anchor

battens: thin strips of fiberglass or wood used to support the roach of a sail

beating to weather: sailing up-wind

bend-on: attaching a mains'l to mast and boom

binnacle: the stand on which the ship's compass is mounted at the helm

bitter end: the very end of a rope

bow: the forward part of a boat

bulkhead: a wall or partition

cabin sole: floorboards, bottom surface of cabin, like the floor of a house

clew: aft corner of a sail

coaming: vertical edge around cockpit or hatch

cockpit: the area from which a boat is steered

davits: crane to lift a dinghy

deck: a horizontal platform on a boat

dinghy: a small boat used to go to and from a larger boat (aka 'a tender')

ebb: the falling tide

fall off: turn away from the wind

flood: the rising tide

foot: the bottom edge of a sail

fore: toward the bow, in front

freeboard: the vertical distance between the gunwales and the water

full press of canvas: sailing with all sails aloft

galley: the kitchen

genoa: large foresail that overlaps the mains'l

ground tackle: the anchor and rode

gunwales (gun'ls): the outer edge of a boat's upper deck

halyard: the line used to hoist a sail

handing the sails: lowering and stowing the sails

hanks: snap hooks for fastening the heads'l to a stay

hank-on: the act of fastening a heads'l to a stay

head: 1) bathroom compartment 2) top of mast 3) top corner of sail 4) the bow

heeling: when a boat leans away from the wind

helm: the wheel or tiller used to steer a boat

hull: the main structure or body of a boat

in irons: a situation whereby a tack is unsuccessful and the boat stops

jib: a heads'l that does not overlap the mains'l

jibing: tacking by turning the stern through the eye of the wind and filling the sails on the opposite side

knot (nautical mile): 1.15 statute miles

lazy jacks: an arrangement of lines which cradle a sail on a boom while not in use

lee shore: the shoreline which lies downwind of a boat; opposite of a weather shore

leech: the rear or trailing edge of a sail

lee helm: when a boat has a tendency to fall off, or turn away from the wind

leeway: the drift of a boat caused by wind

listing: when a boat leans due to damage or improper stowage of cargo

luff: the forward edge of a sail

luffing: when a sail flaps in the wind

mains'l (mainsail): the large sail attached to the main mast and boom

making sail: raising the sails when getting underway

midships (amidships): midway between the bow and stern

mizzen: the smaller mast and sail at the rear of a boat

neap tide: a period of moderate tidal ranges which occur when the Earth, moon, and sun are not in alignment; the opposite of a spring tide

off the wind: away from the eye of the wind, sailing downwind

overhead: the upper surface of a cabin, like the ceiling of a house

preventer: a line or rigging used to prevent an accidental jibe

pointing: when a sailboat is sailing close to the wind

port: 1) the left side of a boat when facing forward 2) a harbor

port holes: a window that can be opened

port lights: a window that cannot be opened

reefing: to reduce sail area in heavy wind

roach: the curved part of a sail that extends beyond a straight line from head to clew

rode: the anchor line made of any combination of chain, cable, or rope

round up: to turn the boat toward the wind

running free: sailing directly downwind

running rigging: lines that are used to raise or adjust sails

scope: the ratio of anchor rode to water depth

sheet: the line used to control the boom and the angle of the sail to the wind

shrouds: fixed cables which support a mast side to side

spring line: a mooring line rigged to prevent a boat from moving fore and aft in a dock

spring tide: a period of extreme tidal ranges which occur when the Earth, moon, and sun are in alignment; the opposite of a neap tide

standing part (of a line): the part of a line that is secure

standing rigging: fixed cables supporting a mast, the combination of stays and shrouds

stays: fixed cables which support a mast fore and aft

starboard: the right side of the boat when facing forward

stern: the rear part of a boat

tack, tacking: 1) the lower, forward corner of a sail. 2) starbord or port tack: the direction from which the wind comes when sailing. 3) turning the bow through the eye of the wind and filling the sails on the opposite side

toe rail: the slightly raised, reinforced edge of the upper deck

topside: on the upper deck

topsides: the part of the hull that is visible above the waterline

transom: the flat vertical surface of the stern

true wind: the wind felt when stationary

underway: when a boat is in motion or not moored

vang: an arrangement of line(s) to prevent the boom from lifting

weather helm: when a boat has a tendency to round up, or turn into the wind

weather shore: the shore which lies to windward of a boat

weigh anchor: raising the anchor in preparation for getting underway

working part (of a line): the part of a line that is being used to tie a knot or secure the line

CPSIA information can be obtained at www.ICGtesting.com
Printed in the USA
BVOW022023101011

273233BV00005B/3/P